OBAMA-RACE, POLITICS, AND
REALITY: AN OPEN LETTER FROM
A BLACK MAN

MAR-RA-RA-BOOKS
Copyright 2011 by Bob Hayes

Ma-Ra-Ra-Books
Calle Mar Egeo 175
Fracc: Costa Verde, Boca Del Rio
Veracruz, Mexico 94294

Library of Congress Cataloging-in-
Publication Data
                Bob Hayes
Obama-Race, Politics, And Reality/
Bob Hayes – 1st pbk. Ed.
1. Hayes, Bob 2. President Obama 3.
Effects of Racism On Politics 4. Role Of
Media

OBAMA-RACE, POLITICS, AND REALITY

BOB HAYES

Life yields only to the conqueror. Never accept what can be gained by giving in. You will be living off stolen goods, & your muscles will atrophy – Dag Hammarskjold

Also by Bob Hayes

"Ten To Call"
"Mexico-A Nation's Culture of Denial"
"Veracruz"
"The River Jordan"
"The Blackbird Quinary"
"For The Love Of A Prince"
"Operation Snowfall"
"Looking For Love In All The Right Places"
"Tequila Changeups"
"As God Is My Witness"

I

OPEN LETTER TO THE
HONORABLE PRESIDENT BARACK
OBAMA:

Dear Mr. President:

Like so many Americans, I was
overjoyed and hopeful when I watched
on TV your taking the oath to become
America's first black president.

I was pleased, thinking you would bring
a fresh vision to remedy the ills of the
prior administration; exited that once
again America would have a president
who could not only read and understand
the Constitution and dribble full-court at
the same time, but charm the world as
he did so.

You would not only find some

resolution to the wars in Iraq and
Afghanistan, but you would begin the
painful economic recovery and restore
America's image around the world.

And while I did not expect you to focus
all your attention on issues of race, I did
breath deeply; confident that finally
there would be someone in the White
House who would acknowledge the
plight of urban America, i.e. the poor
and those whose access to the American
dream was yet unfulfilled.

While I recognized your status as an
Afro-American of mixed race, unlike
some, I was not perturbed,
understanding that this has been a reality
in Black-America since the first slave
owners bedded their female slave
'properties'…that being of mixed blood
did not prevent previous black
Americans like W.E.B. Du Bois and
Walter White from recognizing the
reality of race in America.

I admired your oratory skills and your
ability to remind those who might not
have understood prior, that we were all
Americans.

Your style, your academic achievements, your mercurial political ascent, caused me to reflect that you were part of the new breed, young generation of Black-Americans; those young blacks who were too young to have experienced the overt racism that existed in some sectors of the country before passage of the Civil Rights bills.

Like my three sons, you read about and listened to those of us who experienced those debasing practices, and nodded your head in understanding why most of us were still a bit distrustful of 'the man.'

You would be the first black presidential candidate who would have a chance to convince white America that you were no racial treat.

They would look at your features, listen to you articulate, take account of your intellect, and conclude that unlike other prominent blacks who had sought their votes, you were not one to constantly remind them that they owed Black America a debt because of their ancestors' misdeeds.

They would stare at their TV screens and discern that there was no Reverend Jesse Jackson or Al Sharpton standing behind you winking and smiling.

They would watch you move to the music and they were relieved when it appeared that you had spent more time dancing at your high school sock hops rather than getting down at the D.C. Armory with James Brown and Wilson Pickett, or under blue lights in the basement.

During your campaign they pondered what would be best for America; the first black president or the first female president.

You see Mr. President, this was a very difficult decision for many white Americans, for the only prototype they had in their historical presidential memory file was male and white.

What they knew though was that President Bush had sold them a bill of goods; that they had placed their confidence in him and all they had to show for it was war, a failing economy, and world disfavor.

While they had voted twice for Bush
and his Republicans, they did so with
reservations; not quite sure that he
measured up to the standards they
expected of a leader of the world's most
powerful nation.

But since enough white Americas had
opted to move to the right since
President Johnson signed his civil rights
legislation and sent Southern Democrats
scurrying to change their registration to
Republican, they felt obliged to deny
Gore and Kerry the opportunity to
occupy the White House with their
'leftist' agendas.

White America had 'suffered' though
the Clinton eight years; having tired of
explaining to their colleagues why they
had voted their wallets and not their
'family values' re-electing Clinton.

Ah, but those of us in the black
community understood quite well. We
knew that despite Clinton's shenanigans
and questions regarding his morality,
money was the decisive factor in his
being re-elected.

We knew that as long as white

Americans sensed they could continue their spending and receiving their credit cards in the mail, even you could have been elected at the time.

Yes Mr. President, as is true of most great things accomplished in our lifetimes, timing is everything.

You appeared a welcome alternative to the 'spend at all cost' Republicans and their hypocritical moral stances.

You strutted with an aura of confidence. You walked hand in hand with a beautiful, intelligent wife; two daughters that any father would gladly fawn over.

I was emotionally drained as I watched you take the oath of office, and as a veteran, I virtually choked with pride when you first strolled out to 'Hail To The Chief.'

Yes Mr. President, you were the nation's hope; the right man for the right time.

II

Now, fast forward.

As I sat at my computer, I wondered if my dreams for you had faded slightly.

Yes, I have no doubt that you are cap-able of turning America around, I just wonder if perhaps my expectations have gone awry.

No, I never anticipated that in two or three years you would be able to undue all the blunders you inherited.

What I imagined was that you would take charge; identify a proper course and set sail…that you would identify where you would draw a line in the sand and not capitulate under Republican/Tea Party/right wing rigidity.

We were all waiting for you to spell out your priorities; those principles you would not swallow simply to get along with your political adversaries.

What I did not expect was that you would seem to underestimate the reality of being black in America.

As I watch you spar with the right wing Republicans, I wonder if you really believe that there was ever the slightest chance that these angry white men and women would consider sitting across the table from you and deliberate on just how they could work with you for the good of all Americans.

Once I heard Mr. Rush Limbaugh vow that he wanted you to fail, and I noted how there was no outcry from white America; no rejection and rushing to swear allegiance to you, I could only say 'oh, oh, here we go again.'

It reminded me of my brief stint as a journalist during the early 70s in San Francisco.

I reflected on the prideful days when I and other black journalist met together in Texas to form the National Association of Black Journalist; how as a founding father I looked forward to great changes in the media arena.

Then I recalled how white journalists on my own newspaper reacted to my being charged by the publisher to even the daily's playing field by recruiting minority reporters and editors to convert the paper into the leading vision of the Pacific Rim.

I remembered how disappointed I was when the publisher/chairman of the corporation's board, bowed to the pressure resulting from white staff members filing a petition to prevent the newspaper from becoming a 'minority tabloid'…how it wasn't important that the recruitment effort targeted only the nation's most experienced black, Asian, and Latino journalist from the most prestigious newspapers, but that the paper remain predominately white in not only its numbers but its news coverage..

Once again I understood that it wasn't about what was good for the newspaper; that despite its San Francisco liberal atmosphere and the crying need for fresh input to reflect the area's racial composition, whites only wanted one thing, to preserve what had always existed…their dominance.

So, naturally when I heard Limbaugh's pledge to white America, I kept my ears open, wondering how the 'unbiased' media would react.

Well they certainly gave Mr. Limbaugh sufficient coverage, but I noticed there was little effort to gauge just what effect his words were having.

I wondered why they, like I, did not suspect that the closet doors of racism were creaking as they began to open and its occupants exited.

Suddenly I began to witness a shift in the media.

Now, those who had previously hailed you as the next coming to fresh sour dough bread, were shifting nervously.

But before I proceed, I have to add a caveat to my conclusions.

Since I have been retired for the past twelve years, living in Mexico, my major access to news is CNN cable, Mexican media, internet, and one Mexican/English daily. Thus my access is somewhat limited.

But then, given CNN's 24-hour news programming, I expect that they offer an adequate news analysis and coverage for me to reach valid judgments.

Consequently, given my political, social, and journalist experiences, I was not dismayed as I watched the rapid switch from 'hail to Obama,' to 'what the hell are we going to do now?'

And the devious Republican senators and congressional delegates seized the opportunity full tilt.

Suddenly the 'liberal/impartial' media was under siege.

Anyone who hinted that President Obama was America's new hope was being reminded that he was not the 'white hope' needed to maintain America's image…that it was time for 'good Americans' to rally and 'take back' their country.

The message and the attacks were clear, and the Republican Party had stepped to the front of the parade. They would stand fast. Anything that President Obama proposed…especially if it might be good for the country, thus enhancing his political image…they would unite in opposition.

Health care? Yes every Republican swore that they recognized the high cost and lack of access for millions of Americans, but they could not afford to have the country give thanks to Obama for making their lives better.

Sure, there would be more Americans covered, less denial of coverage by the powerful insurance industry, and no, grandma would not have a death panel deciding her fate.

But what the Republicans initiated was a campaign to repudiate your achievement …one that no president since Truman could accomplish…and denounce your health care program as 'socialism,' another example of the government interfering in the lives of American citizens…getting between them and their doctors.

And if one were to believe the polls that the media relies on to verify its positions, Americans bought the

Republican propaganda hook, line, and sinker!

Then when your administration decided it needed to bail out the nation's cities, banks and auto industry with your emergency stimulus package, again the 'we have no agenda' Republicans went on the offensive, charging that you and your 'czars' were 'meddling' in matters that should be left to big business and the 'people' to resolve these issues.

It didn't matter that the banks and Wall Street, as well as the auto industry, were on life supports, and hundreds of thousands of Americans were on the verge of losing their jobs…that without the stimulus injection the economy would only have suffered more…that with it, thousands of teachers, firemen, and policemen would stay on the job.

What the Republicans needed to show its constituents and those who had voted for you but were now wavering in the breeze, was that the Obama administration had gone astray; that it was another attempt to take over private industry…that it was 'un-American' to interfere in big business…that spending was out of control.

And as they plotted to unseat Democrats
during the mid-term 2010 congressional
and state and local elections, they would
spend billions of unidentified corporate
dollars (thanks to the Republican
Supreme Court) to ensure that
Americans remembered what Limbaugh
had said.

So, once again I checked in on the
media; hoping to find some balance.

Instead what I found was a white-
dominated media bolting for cover.

Now they and their news directors were
in need of 'balanced coverage.'

Whenever the Republican attacks came,
they would extend themselves to ensure
that neither Limbaugh nor the Senate
and Congressional minority whips and
Party leaders accused them of not being
tough enough on you and your allies.

So what to do, they pondered?

Ah, it was time to develop a new
strategy; seek safe haven.

There would be tougher questions for
your administration's spokespersons. If
a Republican and Democrat were on the
air offering their views on America,
CNN would be careful not to appear to
give the Democrats a free lunch.

If there was a strong Republican attack,
charging the Democrat's position as
'radical left wing liberal,' there would
be no reminder that the Republican
position was 'radical right wing
conservative.'

Past CNN hosts like the illustrious Lou
Dobbs would gladly adopt any Fox
network lead. Any position or action
taken by the Administration or groups in
its camp would be smeared with the
label… 'radical leftist.'

But if some Republican-based
organization or politician was under
scrutiny for some questionable action,
the words 'radical right wing' would
suddenly be inappropriate in defining
the person or organization.

So, for example, Fox's/Limbaugh's
attacks against the voter registration
organization Acorn, would be preceded

by the label 'left wing radicals.'

But when the media referred to the Tea
Party, it would be more respectful.
Reference to the Tea Party would not be
preceded by 'right wing radicals.'

If Al Sharpton mentioned that race
might have played a role in some
incident when a policeman fired bullets
into the body of some young black male,
he was 'playing the race card.'

But now, if someone in a Tea Party rally
appeared with a sign depicting the
President of the United States in
demeaning white face, or suggesting he
was akin to a monkey, the Tea Party
participant was merely 'exercising his
freedom of speech,' not playing the race
card.

And while CNN was tarring those 'left
wing radicals' at Acorn with their brush;
suggesting that it and its directors were
guilty of illegal voter registration
practices, and demanded Acorn be
investigated, no attempt was made to
distinguish the action of some out of
work guy hustling to get paid for each

person he registered from that of
Acorn's directors.

CNN, like Fox, seemed not the least bit
concerned.

After all, it was clear that Acorn was not
registering too many Republicans in the
Bible Belt or the deep South.

So when the cry came out to have
Congress cut off funding and the
Republicans acted, the media went to
bed at night confident that they had been
fair, impartial.

Yes, the media needed to show more
'balance.' It needed to prove to the
right wing Republicans that they were
not Obama cronies.

They needed to let the Republicans
know that unlike the media zealot who
admitted swooning during your
campaign, that he was captivated by
your political aura, they were
'professional, impartial,' journalists.

And how to do so? Simple. They
merely needed to remind themselves
what was at stake.

So I found nothing rare in this reversal.
After all, I reminded myself, what was
the difference between those Republican
attack dogs and the media they were
now holding hostage?

Not much.

These media personalities had not only
come under attack from the right wing,
but as well, associates who questioned
their social values as they sipped
martinis over lunch or huddled in
political parleys at social events.

What to do, they asked themselves?
Could they jeopardize becoming
persona non grata by appearing to be
bewitched by a black president?

Wasn't it rather unprecedented and
asking a bit much for anyone to imagine
whites losing face with their
contemporaries/family/friends/media
associates, etc. in defense of some black
president with a funny name like
Obama?

Only on rare instances in historical
America would these 'impartial' media
personalities recall whites risking

reputations and careers for a black.

Those who did hark back and recaptured
a bit of their history remembered a guy
named John Brown who thought he
might help some 'radical' slaves revolt.

But then they recalled how he had ended
up being labeled 'crazed,' and with a
rope around his neck as he stared up into
the heavens.

And since they had never had to
consider the effects a black president
would have on them and the country
before you Mr. President, there was
nothing in their cultural backgrounds or
psychology books to guide them.

All they knew was that as long as there
had been an independent America, the
only face they had seen standing behind
the Presidential seal or the desk in the
Oval Office, had been that of a white
male.

Now reality began to set in.

Media personalities went home, looked
in the mirror, and to their amazement,
realized that much like the Republicans

that they had previously considered a bit
too conservative for their taste, they too
were white!

They too were beginning to realize that
it was too much to swallow. They too
were beginning to wonder if perhaps the
nation had gone too far…that maybe it
was time to 'take back their country.'

Now they were entrenched.

When they needed to seek out public
opinion on such issues as healthcare,
bail-outs, the economy, jobs, whether
you were really an American, that you
were most likely a Muslim, a
socialists…then they would go where
they would find some accord.

Suddenly in order to reflect the mood of
the nation, CNN and the media sent
their reporters to little towns in mid-
America that one needed a AAA map to
locate.

And to make sure that they received the
'balance' reactions they sought, what
better place than in the South or the
Bible Belt?!

No, they would not need to send
reporters and camera crews to such
locales as New York, Chicago, Los
Angeles, San Francisco, Atlanta, Seattle.

They already knew the liberal opinions
of the majority of those residing in
urban America.
And besides, weren't they likely to find
a bunch of non-whites and Jews?

This was not the 'real' America that
Sarah Palin spoke of when she
proclaimed it was time to 'retire' Harry
Reed, Nancy Pelosi, and Obama.

These urban havens were where one
found blacks, Latinos, Jews, Asians, and
too many white liberals.

What CNN needed was a response from
'real' Americans; those who were under
siege from the policies of Obama, Reed,
Pelosi and the Democrats.

What they wanted to avoid was anyone,
anywhere, who might suggest that race
was playing a factor in white America's
strong opposition to you Mr. President.

III

For the first time since I learned to read and stared at 'white only' signs in stores…having to order a hamburger from the 'colored only' window in the alley…sitting in the rear of a trolley car…waiting in 'colored' classrooms for 'new' books to arrive after the school district handed down used ones once the white schools received new ones… relocating and having my white teacher explain that I would be 'better off studying something more practical' than pursuing a college prep agenda…I was now experiencing white America insisting that race was no longer a factor in American society.

The media paved the way, carefully skirting any viable discussion of race and its effects on today's political/social reactions to their new president.

Even as late as September, 2011, when the likes of Morgan Freeman and the Harvard law professor, Randall Kennedy, appeared on CNN and assured that the strong opposition to you is tainted by racism, the news programming went deft.

There would be no need for CNN to assemble a roundtable of experts on race to discuss the issue.

Besides, CNN and major media had its own 'experts' who would assure America that while there may be a few who still clung to such racial views, the majority of Americans rejected such accusations…that the greater majority of Americans did not harbor racial repudiation against the President…that their lack of confidence was based on your inability to live up to the expectations they had set for you.

Suddenly the Tea Party had become the criterion for understanding exactly what agonized all America.

Jobs, less government, states rights, adherence to the Constitution, runaway spending, dismantling the Obama health care plan, protecting the 'American' way of life, family values, were the answers to solving the nation's ills. You and your 'reckless' spending was spiraling the country into a debt that would burden future generations. And the fact that America's economic woes were due in great part to the 'trickle down' philosophies of ex-President Reagan and his Republican successors in the White House, mattered none. There would be no need for America to look back in the mirror to make sure it did not repeat failed economic policies.

To do so would mean a re-examination of the 'beloved Great Communicator' that all Republicans were now quoting as the model the world needed to 'revive' America and restore it to its status of Cold War power.

And while the Tea Party declared that it was not obligated to or under the influence of either sitting Republicans or Democrats, it seemed odd that everything they advocated meshed so smoothly with what Limbaugh and the Republicans were screaming about

Each day CNN and the other media felt it needed to remind us that your popularity was 'eroding,' simultaneously admitting that your approval numbers were higher than many previous presidents in their first two years.

They made sure that we recognized that the Independents who they say were responsible for electing you, had now shifted and favored Republicans.

But what CNN analysts avoided like the plague was admitting that these 'so called' Independents were nothing more than Republicans in sheep clothing; that perhaps the main reason they had voted for you in the first place was out of frustration with the Bush Administration and the Republican Congress whose policies were beginning to devalue their stocks and jeopardize their ability to augment their wealth.

So when polls suggested these 'Independents' were preparing to revert back to their Republican roots, the media hyped it up.

What they needed to illustrate was that
you Mr. President, were in jeopardy;
that because of your inability to walk on
water and perform miracles in your first
few years, you were destined to be a one
term president.

Because of your 'failure' to understand
and respond to the needs of 'real'
Americans, you would to be taught a
swift lesson.

Mr. President, nothing you have done or
will ever do to rescue America from the
Bush policies will suffice as far as your
political opposition is concerned.

If you want to take your wife to a New
York show, you're being extravagant;
another example of reckless spending.

And how dare you and the First Lady
arrive in fashionable attire?

Where was the handkerchief in your
back pocket and her bandana and apron?

After all, who do you think you are, the
President of the United States?!

And if that didn't work, then they could charge you with wasting the 'peoples' money, traversing around the country using Air Force One and Secret Service Agents to take your wife for a night out on the town in of all places, New York! Well, no matter that it wasn't Air Force One and that by law you can't go to the bathroom without Secret Service and the guy with the box and the keys strapped to his wrist, standing outside the door.

The First Lady and daughter taking a trip to Europe?

What's this all about? Who does she think she is, Jackie O.?

And aren't you and your family supposed to live just like 'Joe the Plumber'?

And these vacations to Hawaii and Massachusetts?

Why do you have to drag the media along with you…impacting on local folks with your large entourages?

Aren't you supposed to go to Rock
Creek Park and barbeque some ribs and
put the watermelon on ice?

Then, also, what right do you have
trying to take credit for your programs?

Why aren't you spending more time
kissing the Republican leadership's a...s
than using 'illegal' tactics to push
through legislation that 'no one' in
America wants?

Didn't you promise us in your campaign
that you would end the bickering and
politics as usual?

Didn't you say you would put a halt to
the influence peddlers using their
millions to sway elected officials?

Instead, your critics say what you're just
trying to convince us of is that the
Republicans are 'obstructionists,' that
their only agenda is 'no.'

Well Mr. President, Republicans by and
large don't want to hear the media
explain that they are determined to
block your legislation...that they have
set a record for filibusters...that they

continue to vote as their big business
lobbyists advise…that their single goal
is to minimize your effectiveness in
order to derail any ideas you might have
of winning a second term.

The plan has been activated, and with
the media's assistance, there will be no
more talk of Bush's negative impact on
the world.

Any ills facing America would be
dropped on your door step. It will be
you President Obama…you alone who
will be held accountable. And if the
right wing won't cooperate, then it's
your fault…your failure of leadership.

IV

So Mr. President, why this sudden emergence of factions like the Tea Party?

Why, if the Tea Party and their right wing allies claim that their major concern is big government spending and interference in their lives, we've never had a Tea Party until now?

Where were these Tea Party members when President Bush was spiraling the country into unprecedented debt…when he turned Clinton's surplus into a massive deficit?

Why didn't they organize when the current Republicans who now say they are ready to curb back spending, were rubber stamping every dollar Bush wanted to spend?

And why do they keep insisting that you need to extend the tax cuts to the rich?

And why doesn't someone in the 'impartial' media challenge them by pointing out that during the Clinton eight years the 'fat cats' paid more taxes, yet the nation's economy was very healthy…that none of the riches of the rich had to apply for welfare…that it was exactly these same tax cuts to the 'fat cats' that existed while Bush was running the country; that few if any of those dollars 'trickled down' to create jobs, but remained in the 'fat cats' pockets or went abroad where cheap labor results in more profit and greater returns on investments?

Oh, excuse me. We shouldn't imply anything negative about 'trickle down' economics since it was the darling policy of that 'great communicator,' President Ronald Reagan, now being hailed by every Republican as the greatest political mind/orator since Cato …the same guy who started America down the economic spiral with his 'cut at all cost' Federal programs and any spending that did not benefit the rich.

And by the way Mr. President, isn't it time you stop quoting and hailing Reagan and give more 'props' to presidents like Clinton, Kennedy, Truman and Roosevelt who actually affected some positive change, rather than Reagan's being responsible for a failed economic policy, and proclaimed for 'tearing down' a wall that Mikhail Gorbachev managed to dismantle without our help?

Even this rich guy Donald Trump who once said he might consider giving you a little competition in 2012, talks about how since President Reagan, the U.S. has lost its respect around the world.

These are the kind of guys you need to be cautious of Mr. President.

The Republicans/former Democrats like Trump who have 'come to realize' that the Tea Party is now America's conscious, and that they are the impetus for Americans to begin to right the wrongs that you and other 'liberals' have imposed on the country, are dangerous.

He reminds us that it was Reagan who
'stood up' to the 'Commies'…that it
was Reagan who demanded the Iranians
release those U.S. captives before he
took office 'or else'…that if Carter had
won, those Americans would still be
wallowing in their Iranian cells.

And without saying as much, Mr.
Trump wants his Republican/
Independent/Tea Party allies to know
that you Mr. President are no Reagan;
that you are the reason the world no
longer 'fears' America.

And while you did take him to the
'woodshed' during that annual media
function, and diffused his charge that
there were still questions swirling
regarding your birthright, consequently
taking him off the media interview A-
list, he and his supporters are still out
there ready to throw more mud in your
direction.

But then like me, you're also a student
of history Mr. President, and I'm sure it
hasn't escaped your memory that while
the world was 'afraid' of the U.S. during
Reagan's years in the White House, as
Mr. Trump and other Reagan worshipers

would like current voters to believe,
they often fail to recall historical facts.

They refrain from mentioning the Iran-
contra scandal that led to Daniel
Ortega's Sandinistas coming to power in
Nicaragua…that despite Reagan's
huffing and puffing, the Sandinistas did
gain control with their 'communist
/socialist' ideology.

And oh, let's not forget that in 1983,
241 U.S. Marines were killed when a
suicide bomb blew up their headquarters
in Beirut…that two days later Reagan
approved the invasion of GRENADA!
…that in 1987 an 'errant' Iraqi missile
killed 37 U.S. sailors aboard the USS
Stark…all incidents that illustrated that
the world was terrified of Reagan, and
that Reagan, in contrast to Carter,
showed his fellow Republican what it
meant to be 'tough.'

And wasn't it during Reagan's watch
that Wall Street crashed in 1987?
…wasn't it in 1983 that real GNP fell,
resulting in the worse decline since
1946?…and wasn't it the same Reagan
with his 'trickle down' economics that

introduced the nation's first $trillion
budget and massive deficits?

What I'm getting at Mr. President, is
that maybe it's time for you to stop
quoting ex-President Reagan.

And why is it that the 'independent'
media hasn't done an analysis of
Reagan's union busting ideology…why
they haven't bothered to connect the
dots tying stalled middle-class income
with the decline of union memberships
and worker advocacy?

What I'm getting at Mr. President, is
that maybe it's time for you to quote
someone other than this 'darling' of the
Republicans who are gearing up to
dismantle everything you've tried to do
to improve America…that you do some
of us a disservice by invoking President
Reagan as an example of what's good
for America; especially those of us of
color.

Now, let me move on to another sticking
point.

Mr. President, do you not have at least a
notion that maybe this fervent right

wing dislike for you has nothing to do
with what you have or have not
accomplished?

I understand your reluctance to 'play the
race card,' thus coming under further
attack from the Republicans and their
media allies, but you're a very
intelligent young man, and I'm sure you
know that swallowing your principles
simply to get along with the opposition
just won't change the fact that these
Republicans have convinced some
Americans that you're not even
American.

I also realize that since I too grew up in
a social environment a bit more liberal
than most Black Americans, but that I
did witness in many sectors of America
an era more restrictive in its overt
racism, that it's possible your views and
mine might vary somewhat regarding
the reality of race and America..

Nothing in my experiences as a Black
American allows me to see America as
simply ONE America.

Yes, I heard your speech during the

Democratic convention when you were
an Illinois state senator, and I remember
your advocating that there was no black
America, no white America…that we
were one America.

But were you aware at the time that
there were people like the Tea Party
who would soon remind you that there
is a 'real' America and that apparently
they don't see people like you and I, as
well as Latinos, Asians, gays, white
liberals, and anyone who doesn't listen
to Rush, as part of 'their' America?

Of course I understand your contention;
your wish that we would all see
America in your vision. But then Mr.
President, that's where reality hits the
old road with the dividing line.

Yes, since my teenage years, I too
experienced growing up in an integrated
environment where overt racism did not
prevail.

Schools were integrated. Dating and
marriage across racial lines was
common in Seattle in those days.

I still have non-blacks among my list of boyhood friends.

I enjoyed playing varsity sports and participating in special academic clubs, despite being only one of five blacks in my high school of over 2,000 students.

And when I went to college, the sparse level of black enrollment remained.

And it wasn't until my graduation that I realized that even in, at the time, in an advanced integrated society, there was another side to the American reality.

It didn't take long for me and other blacks in Seattle to realize that, yes, one might marry the white boss' daughter, but working in a white collar position in his company was another thing.

What this environment did was prepare me to understand very well reality of race in America.

I had no doubt that because of my competing in a vastly white dominated academic circle, some whites were indeed fair and sociable, some indifferent, some clearly not wanting to

have any association with the likes of
me.

I recognized that that some of my peers
were excellent students, most average,
some totally intellectually challenged,
and that I could hold my own.

Thus, as I ventured out in life in pursuit
of fulfilling my own dreams, I was
neither awed by, nor contentious in the
presence of non-blacks.

Hobnobbing socially or interacting in
business with whites and others on all
economic levels was as common as
eating over chopsticks with my family's
former next door Chinese neighbors.

But then, Mr. President, I never forgot
later living and working in Los Angeles
and having a white policeman stop my
car, humiliating me by having me
spread-eagle over the hood of my auto,
then before telling me to 'move on boy,'
reminding me that he was 'having a bad
day.'

Had I not understood that he was just an
unpolished, racist member of the force
and not necessarily exemplifying the

entire Los Angeles police department, I
might have done exactly what he wanted
me to do…reacted emotionally and gave
him an excuse to take out his rage; me
ending up in jail on charges of
'assaulting a policeman and resisting
arrest.'

Neither did I forget arriving in Los
Angeles in the 60's and checking rentals
in surrounding suburbs (hoping to find
an apartment near my new job) only to
have doors slammed in my face and a
white co-worker reminding me that I
was looking in the wrong
neighborhoods…that those communities
were predominantly white families
whose folks had migrated from
Oklahoma and Texas during World War
II…people not yet willing to rent to
blacks, Mexicans, Jews, or Asians.

What I'm getting at Mr. President is that
most of us black Americans have
experienced integration. The difference
is that some of us have also experienced
enough racism along the way to
understand that while it would be ideal
to believe that there was only one
America, in our travels we saw enough
to give us doubts that all is yet well.

We still suspect that while the majority of the young Americans of all colors may have had some positive experiences in matters of race, there are still millions of white Americans having a difficult time discarding their racist views.

Oh sure, there are signs of change. The mere fact that you were elected is evidence that times have improved.

But then where do these Tea Party signs come from if not from the closets of racism that were never really extricated of their evil intent?

V

What is a President to do?

Mr. President it seems you have two
choices. You can continue on the road
as a conciliator; hoping that one day
your Tea Party/Republicans
/Independents will eventually concede
and recognize you as 'their'
President…or you can roll up your
sleeves, battle, and do what's right.

You can try to please all the people or
you can be like Lyndon Johnson and say
'to hell with political longevity' and
kick some ass.

Sure you're going to infuriate millions if
they realize that you're black after all;
that just like Jackson and Sharpton, you
sense that blacks, Latinos, the poor, and
gays are getting stiffed.

But then haven't you already sent the
right wing and their Tea Party zealots
into a tizzy by simply showing up on
TV?

What is there to lose?

If they won't agree to sit at the same
table and salute you, then why keep
inviting them to dinner?

If every time they hear 'Hail To The
Chief' and see you walk out as
Commander-In-Chief…watch their boys
in uniform have to salute as you pass by
with the American flag hoisted, and they
grasp at their heart and curse, then what
do you expect you can do to make them
love you?

If the Independents who claimed they
voted for you now realize that you can't
part the Red Sea…forget walking on
it…and are now returning to their
Republican base, weren't you a bit
suspicious why they punched your name
on their 2008 ballots?

Didn't it ever cross your mind that
maybe it wasn't because they were
overwhelmed with your oratory skills,

your good looks, or your intelligence?

Was there ever a moment when you asked yourself… "are these folks looking for an alternative to Hillary because they just can't stand women in power?"… "maybe they're just pissed off at George B. for taking them for a ride in his pickup truck?"

Sure they bragged how they too had decided it was time for America to do the right thing; put the first black into the White House. But then when they realized you were only human; that the two term debacle of Bush had left the country with a mountain of disorder that not even God would have asked his son to rectify in one swift breathe, they took out their disappointment on you.

Some of these Independents/ Republicans are intelligent folks Mr. President. They know that it is impossible to bring the country back to the prosperous Clinton era overnight

They can see the world changing and that know that the global order will never be the same with China, Japan, India, Brazil, Germany, France, and others challenging, and globalization being the way of the future.

But they cast their votes for George Bush anyway and fought to ensure that no Gore or Kerry would defeat him.

When it appeared Al Gore had won the popular vote and that there may have been some questionable vote counting going on in Florida, they were confident that the Republican dominated Supreme Court would come to the rescue.

And when Senator Kerry made his challenge, the Republican machine pulled out all its ammo.

Their favorite son, President Bush, had been branded by some on the left as less than a war hero; maybe even a deserter for being AWOL in the Air Guard while other patriotic airmen were trying to elude North Vietnamese ground to air missiles and not end up being checked into the Hanoi Hilton.

But not to worry, the Republican strategists had something for the American voters to chew on.

By simply reversing the message, Kerry,
a decorated war hero who had dodged
enough Vietcong bullets to know that
war was hell, was suddenly on the
defensive.

He had become the villain; one whose
bravery in combat was being
questioned.

Didn't he return and become an anti-war
advocate?

Wasn't that enough to discredit him as
an American patriot?

Suddenly any documentation suggesting
Bush might have been missing in action
disappeared.

No records could be found to
substantiate that the President might
have 'cut and run.' And if anyone came
forth with such charges, CNN and other
media outlets had already reached their
conclusion… 'insufficient evidence.'

But the 'swift boat' ad attacks against
Kerry would continue rolling across TV
screens until enough American voters
were convinced that America didn't

need another New England 'liberal'
Democrat in the White House with a
rich wife whose ketchup and pickles
they actually loved.

But you see Mr. President, the
Republicans always figure that
Democrats want voters to see them as
being above playing dirty. They bank
on Democrats striving to be viewed as
politicians who prefer to play fair.

So when they attack Kerry and other
Democrats with misinformation, they
know that there are sufficient voters out
there who'll believe the first ad they see
or sound bite they hear…that most are
looking for any iota to reinforce long
held biases and socio/political stances.

Unlike those on the left and the center-
left, these right wingers could care less
if the garbage they spew has any
validity. What they simply want is to
win, no matter their methods.

So, Mr. President, exactly what do you
think they'll have in store for you as you
look forward to the 2012 presidential
election?

Are you thinking that maybe, just
maybe there has been a change of heart;
that this Republican right wing and their
Tea Party henchmen are planning a
birthday party to show you some love?

Well Mr. President, a bit of advice.

If you think the mud they slammed
against Senator John Kerry would have
drawn an unsportsmanlike flag, or
maybe an ejection from an NFL referee,
then I suggest you do like the old
Oakland Raiders and put something
special inside the old adhesive tape
before you take the field.

You'll wake up one morning during the
campaign and see yourself on TV ads
wrapped in African garb, speaking
Swahili…notice that your skin has
suddenly darkened as the ads show you
being hugged by Jesse Jackson…
suddenly realize that in your 'dark' past
there was another white woman in your
life, except this one claims you
impregnated her during one of your wild
pot smoking adventures… that your
'illegitimate son,' 'Jomo Obama,' is
now somewhere in Kenya revitalizing
the Mau Mau movement…staring at ads

showing you in an Indonesian school room in white robe and turban, watching the late Bin Laden assemble a bomb.

So I suggest Mr. President that you come out swinging.

As soon as the Republicans and their Tea Party allies spend their millions slipped into their coffers by corporate America, I hope you'll have your own ads and messages armed and ready.

The first time they show an ad on CNN and Fox depicting you in Nazi uniform, you need to make sure your Republican candidate does not come across as Jimmy Stewart…more like a Dixiecrat in the traditional white robe and hood.

And I hope you won't procrastinate when CNN charges you with 'playing the race card' while they ignore Tea Party signs labeling you a racist.

And for sure Mr. President, don't be persuaded by the polls that CNN will post daily in hopes they can sway your opponents to come out and vote, simultaneously letting your supporters believe that all is lost, no need to vote.

Just understand Mr. President that this has nothing to do with your performance, those things you have or have not accomplished.

There is simply a segment within the 50 states that can't accept the changing times.

What they want is a return to the 'good old days' when everything positive and American was the same reflection they had when they looked in the mirror.

Hey, some of these right wingers are pining for the 1950s when everything on TV was white except for Rochester… when they could buy a plywood, one-level in suburbia sans neighbors of color…when their kids didn't bring home rap music…when, if they earned $2,000 a month they could have a 'colored' servant.

Recognize that there are still millions out there who not only want to see blacks back on billboards gnawing on watermelons without someone suggesting the ad was racist.

Realize that while the nation may have
grown accustomed to seeing Donavan
McNabb/Michael Vick reaching under a
white centers butt, they still think
Peyton Manning is smarter.

And while they all claimed they agreed
with the polls that General Powell was
the most popular man in America, they
sighed relief when he declared he
would not seek the presidency...kind of
snickered while they watched
Bush/Cheney/Rumsfeld send Powell up
to the U.N. with photos of labs on
wheels that surely contained evidence of
Hussein's evil intent.

These are not people who go to bed each
night praying that God show them the
moral path Mr. President.

If they do pray each night, these
Republicans and their supporters hope
that God will show them how to get rid
of you and your band of black, Latino,
and gay supporters.

They don't worry much about the young
whites who voted for you in numbers, or
the white women who did likewise.

They trust that as history has shown,
most of these kids will one day don their
Brooks Brothers suits and see the light.

Whether the women will is irrelevant.
After all, there are enough Sarah Palins
now to counter any liberal white women
still swooning over you Mr. President.

You see, I noticed that when you took to
the road in mid-August, 2011, with your
'Middle America Bus Tour,' the media
and the opposition were ready.

A CNN news host wanted to know if
maybe you shouldn't be back in the
Oval Office trying to find jobs for
Americans…taking his cue from Mitt
Romney, who said you were more
concerned with 'saving your job rather
than finding jobs for others.'

And some guy with a funny name like
Reince Priebus who chairs the
Republican National Committee, even
said you were out on the road trying to
feed Americans 'dog food' disguised to
make us think it was good for us.

You see Mr. President, they've already
drawn up their game plan, and every

time you step outside your bedroom
they're going to let the American public
know that you're not leading…that
voters need to make a right turn to right
the nation.

VI

So what about the rest of America Mr.
President; the ones the right wing long
dismissed as 'not really American?'

What can you do to make sure blacks
continue to come out and vote?

What can you do for the Latino
community to prevent more of them
from signing up with the Republicans
(remember, they gave that guy Bush
40% and McCain 35%)?

Why are the gay voters a bit
uncomfortable with you lately?

Well, as one of those blacks who sought
out your name on election day, I can
speak for what I imagine some in the
community wish you would do.

You see Mr. President, since I never felt I could look myself in the mirror the next morning if I had swallowed my principles to get along in the media world, and not now having to consider any negative fallout for any opinions I might have that may alienate those who disagree, I am able to speak my mind and maybe throw in a few reflections for others less unimpeded.

So as I note how silent black journalists are now, I simply suspect most don't want to be accused of piling on.

They see you under daily attack and decide it's best not to throw gasoline on the fire.

These young black journalists may not have experienced disapproving glares when they first walked into their newsrooms like many of us old timers, but they know that something is askew as they watch their white counterparts chomping at the bit in anticipation of your fall.

They ache because they too are under great pressure. They need their jobs in this time of joblessness, and they are hesitant to take to their computers and let the American public know that they and their fellow blacks are hurting as well.

They would like to remind you Mr. President that while the nation's unemployment hovers near 8%, there are too many in the black urban centers whose unemployment has soared to some 30%, and who wouldn't know how to fill out a job application correctly if one arrived in their mail slot.

These young, black journalist would like to ask you if you have anything in store for their community; whether there is some kind of urban plan that will deal with the need for rebuilding the nation's infrastructures, schools…that maybe you have up your sleeves some sort of Urban Peace Corp that will reward some of America's young gung ho college grads who can't find a job, with an opportunity to lend a helping hand to some of the less fortunate…maybe some program that will induce some of our rich athletes and entertainers to show up and be role models for kids looking for a sense of direction…that maybe just like your Justice Department/DEA/ATF

/FBI coordinate to bust hundreds of drug
cartel members selling poison to our
kids, you can convince them to put
together a few operations that would
relieve cities like Chicago and New
Orleans, and help them rid themselves
of the gangs and criminals that inhibit
our kids ability to walk to and from
school safely.

Just a thought Mr. President. And while
I realize there are those in the political
arena and those sitting in front of their
TVs slurping down their six-packs who
will insist that you be impeached for
such 'radical,' 'socialist' actions, I think
most Americans would applaud you and
say 'about time.'

And I'm sure black Americans would be
putting on the old 33 1/3 Marvin Gaye
vinyl hits "What's Going On," and
"Inner City Blues" and raising their fists
high.

You see Mr. President, these are the
blacks who turn on their TVs and see
you in town hall and back yard meetings
surrounded by mostly whites, and
wonder when you're going to show up

in Harlem, Watts, or the South Side of
Chicago.

They know in their hearts that you
understand the plight of black America,
they just wonder if one day you're going
to snub your nose at the Republicans
and declare 'black is beautiful.'

What had them scratching their heads
Mr. President, was hearing you
admonish the Congressional Black
Caucus and guests at their annual
meeting in 2011.

They couldn't understand why you
chose this event to remind us to 'stop
complaining…get to work.'

What they couldn't ever recall was your
berating your white audiences to 'stop
complaining.'

Black folk understand that you are the
President of all Americans and that your
world-wide responsibilities far outweigh
those of a single community or ethnic
group. They just wish once in a while
they could get a little more love from
you.

History also tells them that it would do
the Republicans and the Tea Party a
great favor if black America would toss
you aside and stay at home when it's
time to vote.

As a matter of fact Mr. President they're
banking on it. It's part of their strategy
to brainwash as many blacks as possible
to abandon you.

And oh, by the way, did you note how
quickly the media threw out that bone of
contention, highlighting how you
berated the Black Caucus at their 2011
annual event…how you told them to
'stop complaining' and 'get to work'

But, unlike when you announced that
the private sector was doing fine i.e. the
economy, the media didn't join with the
Republicans and take you to the
woodshed for making what they
perceived a blunder…not accuse you of
a faux pas.

They got the reaction they knew would
come from Congresswoman Maxine
Waters and others who needed to
remind you that they not only have been
supporting you through thick and thin,

but that they've been on the front line of
the movement long before you entered
the White House.

But the media had no interest in
examining just how you relate to the
plight of Black America, only to make
sure that white America realize that
'even some blacks are questioning your
ability to lead.'

You can bet on it Mr. President. By the
time they finish reviewing and
approving their negative ads, you're not
even going to be black anymore!

And as soon as you counter by saying
"yes I am," they're going to make sure
that the media folks chalk that up as
another case of you playing the 'race
card.'

So like you, most blacks are in a bind
Mr. President.

They understand the dilemma you're
faced with and they realize that with the
defrocked Michael Steele…that new
young black Republican from Florida,
Alan West…that guy Herman Cain who
became delusional, thinking he could

garner enough Tea Party/right wing
votes to take you on come 2012… plus
an occasional black 'conservative'
showing up on TV cheering on the
Republicans and predicting your
fall…Hank Williams Jr. labeling you
'the enemy,' and 'Hitler,' before
declaring he was 'misquoted,' you don't
need any more black rejection.

And now that Mr. Cain scheduled to
host his own right-wing talk
show/Obama lynching air time, you can
bet he'll come out with guns blazing;
hoping to assure all of his white friends
that you're just a Reverend Wright
surrogate intent on making white folks'
lives miserable.

And your fellow black supporters?

They know that what you need now is
some black love, but then Mr. President,
so do they.

What they witness when they open their
newspapers or turn on to CNN, is an
administration on the defense.

They wonder if maybe some of your
advisors are cautioning you to avoid

tossing further raw meat for the
Republicans and Fox to gnaw on if they
see you within five hundred feet of the
black community.

They find it difficult to understand that
if you're really serious about the jobs
and education situation in America, why
the urban center would not be the initial
focus of your efforts; why they see you
berating blacks at the Black Caucus
function, but never chastising the rest of
America when you're speaking to
mostly white and Latino groups.

But then when they don't see you
standing amid a crowd of black folks
except at NAACP and Urban League
conventions, and when black
Congresspersons invite you to dine with
them, they wonder if maybe their
definition of black differs slightly from
yours.

You have to understand Mr. President,
Black-America is not accustomed to
having one of their own in such a
position of power.

They may forget from time to time that
while you are one of them, you are not

them; that being President is not a communal thing but an awesome responsibility that none of us ever conceived as we were growing up and dreaming how we too could get a slice of the American pie.

Like many white Americans, many blacks are a bit befuddled as well, however for different reasons.

A sizeable segment of the white community wishes you would go away so they can once again see one of their 'good ole boys' in the Oval Office.

They want 'their' America back and you Mr. President, are symbolic of the threat to 'their' America the news media is constantly hinting about.

Meanwhile blacks just want to hold on to you a bit longer. They want to one day say to their kids and grandkids that once there was this great man who came at a time of great turmoil and righted the ship that made America once again a nation that all would be proud of.

They want to make sure that white America not dismiss you as a mere

deviation from the norm; a political
meteor that burned out before reaching
its goal.

It is a difficult task Mr. President but I
and millions of others count on you.

But some of us are wondering if you
have drawn a line in the sand that
illustrates where the buck ends…what it
is you're unwilling to compromise on?

We've witnessed your successes…how
you saved the country from falling over
Niagara Falls financial abyss…how you
got that health deal through…how you
kept those Republicans in Washington
just before Christmas/New Years and
got your repeal of 'Don't Ask, Don't
Tell; that S.A.L.T. arms treaty with
Russia, and some other bills
passed...how you were the one who
rendered Osama Bin Laden and Al-
Awalaki passé; fulfilled ex-President
Bush's Old West proclamation…
"Wanted, Dead or Alive"…except you
changed your wanted poster to read
simply "Dead."

But we're still in need of a 'heads up'
on just where you're going to put up

your blockade that will cause McCain
and his bunch to cower and go back into
their reactionary silos.

You see Mr. President, if we knew, for
example, that those right wingers were
confident that you would not budge
when they try to get you to sign a bill
sending black folk to Liberia, we'd go to
bat for you…even take to the streets if
necessary.

We believe you have the right stuff to
turn this county around and put it on a
course that will make us all proud to say
we were there…that we witnessed your
great feats.

But you had us scratching our heads
over this latest debt ceiling debacle.

We heard you remind one of the upstart
Congressional Tea Party darlings to not
challenge you, but once you got them to
vote to raise the ceiling, it wasn't you
raising a black glove in victory.

What we heard was the Republican
leaders reminding their cast of Tea Party
congressmen that they had won!

Suddenly they and their allies were
cracking jokes on TV, suggesting that
Americans understood that to
'compromise' meant 'weakness.'

And then we didn't hear those media
spokespersons reminding America that
to compromise was politically
advantageous.

Suddenly Democrats were on TV with
lowered heads, implying that you had
'blinked' in the face of the Republican's
salvo…that instead of holding firm on
your insistence to have the richest of the
rich pay more taxes…that you would
sign no legislation that placed the
burden on the backs of the poor and the
middle-class…you caved.

Now we don't see you on the basketball
court attacking your opponents,
illustrating your aggressive nature.

When we see you now you appear on
the defensive, with the Tea Party
charging in your direction.

You even gave Herman Cain a reason to
declare his own brand of 'blackness,'
asserting that the reason we don't vote

Republican is because we've been
'brainwashed'…that he was going to get
ONE THIRD of the black vote!

And I'm still waiting for the media to do
a little fact checking as they like to do
on some issues…to record which party,
Democrats or Republicans, has
historically been in the forefront of what
progress Black Americans have made
since WWII.

But don't get me wrong Mr. President,
we still have your back. We just need to
see you block a couple of Tea Party set
shots…maybe get whistled for an
intentional foul.

VII

There are those waiting in the wings for
you to stumble and fall Mr. President,
and not all are eligible to vote for you.

There is a nation south of your border,
for, example, that wants the world to
believe you have deceived them.

Each day in their media they question
whether you have betrayed them by not
opening your borders to allow illegal
immigrants to flee from their homes;
why you have not forced your Congress
to pass some kind of legislation to halt
the flow of arms from the U.S. into
Mexico.

A word of caution Mr. President.

Remember, just as you have your own
internal issues prioritized, so do those in
Mexico.

You see Mr. President, whether you are successful in other aspects of your presidency is of little concern for those south of the border.

What they care about can be summed up in two words… 'illegal immigration.'

Mexican politicians and the rich and powerful clearly understand that next to the annual approximate $47 billion derived from their precious Pemex petroleum industry to fill Mexico's revenue coffers, the some $21 billion in remittances from those Mexicans living and working in the U.S., is the country's second greatest source of revenue…that tourism (mostly American) is their number three source of income…that fourth are the goods and products they send flowing into the U.S. market.

They are well aware that without those billions annually being remitted by illegal and legal Mexicans working in the U.S., plus the tourism and trade, Mexico's economy would tank.

So, no matter the cost to the American tax payer or any socio/political impact resulting from the flow of illegal immigrants across the Rio Bravo, it's the money that drives the propaganda.

If 400 Mexican illegal immigrants perish trying to swim across the Rio Bravo, or die of dehydration in the Arizona desert, it is the U.S.' fault, not those who pay thousands to 'coyotes' in a desperate trek to improve their lives.

And Mr. President, I hope you're not holding your breath waiting for Mexico to spend its dollars and manpower to discourage some 12% of its population from fleeing across the border.

They have reminded you that they see no need to have such a thing as a border patrol that might impede the flow of their poor into the U.S.

After all, why should they take money from their treasury to discourage some exodus needed to keep the pockets of their rich 'criollos' filled?

And of course they are going to point the finger at you each time some 'Zeta,' narco-traffic killers gun down their

police, elected officials, fellow drug
traffickers, or innocent bystanders.

It will be your fault…your
unwillingness to stand up to Congress
and the NRA to stop guns from crossing
the Mexican frontier.

It will be your inability to stop
Americans from snorting so much coke
and smoking so much marijuana.

You see Mr. President, no matter how
many blacks and Mexicans and
Mexican/Americans are sent off to
prison disproportionately to whites for
drug related violations…no matter how
many of our jails are filled to capacity
because of petty drug dealers being
imprisoned… the authorities and
politicians down here have convinced
their fellow Mexicans that your police
and DEA are simply sitting on their
hands while the snorting and smoking
goes on.

And if they do mention in the media in
Mexico that your Attorney General
announced a major drub bust, and it just
happens that the 600 people rounded up
are of Mexican descent, the feeling is

that just like your increased deportation of illegal immigrants, you're being selective, only hunting down Mexicans who are simply in the U.S. to work and support their families back in Mexico.

You see Mr. President, to further examine drug trafficking in the U.S. just might implicate too many of these 'innocent' illegal immigrants as major players in the distribution and sell of drugs in the U.S....that there actually exists a Mexican Mafia in the U.S. that is responsible for a large portion of the drug trafficking.

Now, Mr. President, how would your allies south of the border explain that some of their expatriates have actually migrated up north to do such a thing?

You see, as far as President Calderon and the power brokers in Mexico are concerned, it's best for their fellow Mexicans to continue doing what historically has served them well… blame the U.S....deny any culpability.

Remember Mr. President, you're dealing with a nation with a cultural history constructed on denial.

While their politicians complain that it
is only the drug snorting and smoking in
the U.S. that is responsible for Mexico's
violent drug wars, isn't it odd that there
is never any mention of the lack of
effort Mexico applies to prevent drugs
from Columbia and other South
American countries to cross its southern
border or enter its ports and airstrips?

When was the last time your people at
NSA or one of your AWAC crews
picked up on one of Calderon's cabinet
ministers hosting a press conference to
warn the people of Mexico of the
increasing usage of drugs internally…
charts showing the percentage of the
Mexican cartels sales and distributions
internally…in Africa, Europe, Asia?

Well maybe it's best to keep pressing
the denial button…not mention local
drug sales and usage…just have
Mexicans thinking that all that cocaine
coming in from South America and
marijuana harvested in Mexico
continues north…that while the cartels
are extorting local businesses,
kidnapping, stealing and reselling
Pemex gas, having federal/state/local
officials in their pockets, these violent

killers prefer not to corrupt their own by selling drugs internally!

Isn't it somewhat of a contradiction when they ask you to stop guns on your side of the border from flowing south, but they do little to make sure these guns don't pass Mexico border check points?

And why is it that the Mexican government regularly holds press conferences to announce the number of guns seizes bearing U.S. registration… the tons of drugs they seize headed north…but never to illustrate what they're doing to boost up their efforts to prevent drugs entering Mexico…to prosecute those involved in taking bribes to allow weapons and drugs to enter their country?

And one more thing Mr. President, would it be illegal for Mexico to use some of those Merida Initiative funds provided by American tax payers to purchase some of those high-caliber assault weapons so their ill-armed police won't have to flee when they see those dark-tinted SUVs sans license plates rolling down their streets with four occupants wearing dark shades?

You would think Mr. President that if only you would arrest every kid puffing on a joint or some rich kids snorting coke in their $5,000 a month apartments, that all of Mexico's problems would end.

If you used the CIA, NSA, Special Ops to assist ATF in locating and prosecuting gun traffickers, there would be no violence in Mexico.

Do you really believe Mr. President that your reluctance to see this external problem for what it truly is will enhance your status with Mexican/American voters?

Do you really believe Mexico's President's coming to the U.S. and vowing that "wherever there is a Mexican is Mexico," would set well if you came down and visited me and announced "wherever there is an American is America?"

It may play well in the U.S. press when you and your fellow Democrats go on record stating that resolving this drug problem is one that both the U.S. and Mexico equally share responsibility for, but you also need to make sure that those south of the border understand that it is not the U.S. that 'demands' that Mexico allow drug dealers to be the middle men and use their country as the base of export.

It is not the U.S. that has made Mexico violent.

And by the way, with so much drug usage and trafficking in the U.S., why isn't there the related violence that we see in Juarez, the states of Leon, Michoacan, Guerrero, Veracruz, and throughout much of Mexico ?

Why are U.S. drug dealers not killing some 10,000 rivals annually in street shootouts in U.S. cities…not attacking local police stations and murdering law enforcement personnel…not gunning down elected officials with impunity…extorting, kidnapping?

What is it about the Mexican culture
that finds it easier to blame others, i.e.
the U.S. for its internal problems rather
than admit that it's their own culture of
corruption and denial that accounts for
its deplorable education system, its
poverty, its violence, its lack of
development?

One word Mr. President… 'denial.'

I'm sure you were given a briefing when
35 bodies were dumped on the city of
Boca Del Rio's busiest street, despite
Veracruz' governor earlier insisting that
'all was calm,' to prove that the cartels
could act how and when they chose.

But maybe you were too busy with
events going on at the 2011 U.N.
opening; when Mexico's President
Calderon was 'pleading' for the
delegates to admonish you for allowing
illegal weapons to enter his country
from the U.S….that if not for the
cocaine snorting and marijuana smoking
Americans, all would be peaceful in
Mexico.

But did he call you Mr. President and
explain that except for one, the 35

bodies dumped the day before, were all strangled; that there were no U.S. guns responsible for the violent deaths?

Or do you think Calderon, like his counterparts, would prefer the world to think that the only reason those killers in Mexico act so violently is because you refuse to take action against U.S. gun dealers and their National Rifle Association ally?

And oh, President Obama, while you're taking time from your busy schedule to peruse this little note, ask someone in your administration to look into the different ways Mexico and the U.S. view their respect for each other's internal affairs.

Maybe ask them why it's ok for some illegal immigrants to march in the streets of Los Angeles and Chicago, waving Mexican flags, demanding their 'rights?'

Then ask them why if I did the same in Mexico I would be extradited within the week and advised not to return, that is after they released me from jail?

Check into why some cities in the U.S. like San Francisco, Chicago, and New York have changed their laws, permitting illegal immigrants to vote in local elections…arguing its justification because illegal immigrants pay taxes, work, and their children attend public schools

Hmm, very interesting. Now I must admit my children are adults and do not live with me or attend Mexican schools, but I assure you I spend an ample amount each month to help support Mexico's economy. And if by some strange quirk I did have children born in the U.S., I assure you they would not be able to attend public schools in Mexico. And under no circumstances can I, even as an 12-year legal resident, vote in Mexico.

But you see Mr. President, Mexico's laws are very clear; state that I not only don't have the right to vote, but that I can't even work in any trade other than perhaps giving English classes or maybe consulting with a foreign company doing business in Mexico..

And by the way Mr. President, Mexico's
constitution is very firm…assures that
no foreigner has rights in Mexico like in
the U.S.

You can live here if your $1,200 peso
visa fee is renewed on time annually,
and you don't get involved in politics
(like waving an American flag in the
streets while you protest and demand
your rights).
While locals who qualify, can obtain a
U.S. tourist visa for approximately the
same equivalent in dollars and only have
to renew it every 10 years!

And for God's sake, don't do or say
anything that may be interpreted as one
'meddling' in the nation's internal
affairs or disrespecting the flag or the
National Anthem!

Maybe you read about the group of
young Mexican/American musicians
(one was the late Selena's brother) from
Texas who came down to Mexico to
perform several years ago and were
warned that if they did not remove the
replica of a Mexican flag that they had
decorated one of their guitars with, they

would be fined and/or jailed if they
refused to do so.

You see Mr. President, it's okay for
sitting Mexican presidents to travel to
the U.S., meet with Mexican expatriates,
and express 'demands' that those
immigrants living illegally in the U.S.
be given their 'rights,' and that the U.S.
treat them equally… 'demand' that the
U.S. adopt immigration reform and
refrain from deporting illegal parents
whose children are legal citizens.

But then Mr. President if you were to
venture on Air Force One down to
Mexico and meet with a group of
American expatriates residing in San
Miguel de Allende, for example, and
made the same demands, and maybe
some suggestion that Mexico open
opportunities for American oil
companies to invest and develop
partnerships with Mexico's Pemex oil
producer, you would be scolded;
reminded that once again America was
'meddling' in Mexico's internal affairs
and trying to use its influence over
'pacifists' Mexico.

So Mr. President, this immigration issue
that so many in the U.S. are
disappointed over because you have not
yet come through with your promise to
pass some type of reform…exactly
what's in it for the rest of us?

Yes, I've read what some pundits are
saying…how immigrant workers are
good for the American economy and the
nation's future…how issues of trade,
immigration, competing with out
sourcing jobs, are all interrelated.

But you see I get confused because
these experts on immigration tend to
usually mix apples and oranges.

I get the value of LEGAL immigrant
workers being inviting to the U.S. to
attend our universities and work in our
industries, especially high-tech, and I'm
aware that each year the U.S. allows
some 85,000 such immigrants into the
country legally…that I did read that
overall, some 2 million immigrants each
year are allowed to enter the U.S.

What I find questionable is why those
who advocate more immigrant workers
prefer not to differentiate between an

ILLEGAL who crossed the Rio Bravo with an average 8th grade education, and a college graduate in engineering from India, or an exchange student from Ghana.

How is it that an illegal coming to America hoping to find a job harvesting fruits or vegetables, or nailing up sheet rock is saving jobs from being outsourced?

How is a South Korean immigrant who's been waiting 10 years to have his application approved, pays thousands of dollars to fly across the Pacific with his family, arrives in Los Angeles with enough cash to open a business, lumped in with an illegal immigrant who pays a 'coyote' $50,000 pesos (some $4,500 U.S. dollars) to tramp through the Arizona desert so he can find a job at McDonald's that pays more in one hour than he can earn in a 10-hour day in a Mexican McDonald's?

Hey, Mr. President, I get it why they come. I know why the churches, special interest groups, small businesses rally for more immigration…they all profit from low wage workers and padding

their numbers to fill their pews and
increase their .political and bargaining
power.

And trust me, if I was born in Mexico
and had to face the sordid lack of
opportunities that exist today in Mexico,
I too would probably find myself
following some 'coyote' across the Rio
Bravo and the Arizona desert.

What I don't get though is why you and
so many fellow Democrats are more
vocal about the need to resolve
Mexico's problems than the problems of
urban America?

What puzzles me is why we have to put
one on the back burner while we stir up
something for the other?

Is it because it's politics as usual Mr.
President?

Hey, I was in total agreement when you
masterminded that Homeland Security
measure through that will temporarily
allow some young illegal kids to not be
deported, but I wasn't shocked when
your 'friends' on the other side of the
Senate and Congressional aisles threw

that 'bean ball' in your direction.

Even Senator Rubio had to admit that
what you did wasn't all bad; simply that,
once again, you overstepped your
Presidential powers (translation…you
out foxed the opposition).

And of course when the howling
Republicans took to the TV shows and
accused you of going around the
Congress and the Senate, the media let
them off the hook.

Where were the media news hosts
reminding your critics that what you had
done was within your legal rights as
President…that there was no edict or
exercise of power…simply a program
revision?

Funny how I didn't here them remind
your critics that you did do a little
'boning up' on the Constitution while
you were hitting the books in
school…that maybe you knew a bit
more about presidential authority that
most of your opponents.

No, what they did was challenge
members of your administration to

respond to the Republican critics that
you had somehow violated the
Constitution…that once again you were
demonstration your 'king' status by
bypassing Congress.

But you had someone in you corner, Mr.
President.
Believe me, I was elated the following
Monday morning when CNN's Soledad
O'Brien (you remember her, the
attractive young, Latina-looking
morning host who shocked Reverend
Jackson once by reminding him that she
too was black) 'sacked' one of your
Republican Congressional 'bully'
critics…offering a chronology of years
of Republican opposition votes to
anything your Administration had
submitted that implied you wanted to
pass a Dream Act or any other
legislation that would allow any young
illegal resident some relief.

After a fit of stuttering, your Republican
Congressman foe, insisted that, no
matter, you still show have submitted
the measure to the Congress so they
could vote against it.

And oh Mr. President, before I move on from my concerns about another nation's priorities, is it possible that you can have someone check on a little matter that would be of great benefit to some American retirees living in Mexico like myself who monthly have deductions taken from their Social Security for Medic Care.

You see, I understand there has been some requests to help us use our Medicare benefits south of the border, but as of yet there has been no action taken on the part of your Administration.

You think while you are trying hard to help illegal immigrants in the U.S. benefit by putting them on a path to citizenship, that the next time you and Calderon or his successor communicate, you can maybe get him to put in a good word with his own Institute of Social Security (IMSS) to allow us to use our Media Care cards in their IMSS hospitals?

That shouldn't be too difficult for you to pull off Mr. President, given the number of illegal immigrant families in the U.S.

getting their welfare checks each month, and being able to be treated in U.S. hospitals without coverage.

And oh, Mr. President, while you are contemplating just how much you're going to ask Congress to spend helping Mexico deal with this drug problem, maybe you need to ponder just what the power brokers south of the border expect of you.

There's this little quote that appeared in a Veracruz daily, attributed to a current Mexican Senator by the name of Rosario Green Marcias that might give you a hint.

She explains that Mexico will not resolve its drug trafficking violence without the U.S.' help but… "the help must be without conditions."

You see Mr. President, what the Mexican politicians insist that you do is send the money but don't stipulate that none of it is misdirected into the off-shore bank accounts of some officials, or maybe spent on a lucrative 'contract' for a brother or cousin.

Maybe you already know this Mr.
President, and perhaps I'm preaching to
the choir as they say, but identifying
responsible agencies down here that
actually investigate and prosecute acts
of corruption and misappropriation are
as difficult to stumble upon as a right
wing Tea Party member who's set to
vote for you come 2012.

Just a little something for you to chew
on Mr. President as you prepare for your
next meeting with Mexico's political
elite.

VIII

Now there's something else I need to
ask you Mr. President

Are we still a Democratic party that
takes the black vote for granted?

Oh sure, I understand that black voters
really don't have options like your
Independent voters who can go back
home to the Republicans if you don't
perform miracles in two or three years.

And I realize that most blacks even
cringe when they watch a Tea Party
candidate at a rally and they see two or
three black faces strategically placed
behind the speaker in TV camera range,
amid the cadre of supporters.

Like most blacks I know there are no
welcome mats out in the Republican,
Tea Party, or Independent factions; that

the few blacks you see in their midst seem to have some kind of identity problem when they are allowed to speak as they attempt to justify their party affiliation. ..

Does Michael Steele have to be so anti-Obama that he can't wonder why he is the only dark face in the room?

And yes I do wonder why, if Republicans are really sincere about seeking to boost their black base, you don't see them spending those mysterious corporate dollars on black Republican candidates for the Senate and governorships, only on a spattering of congressmen and some guy who never held office but thinks he can be a better black president…all black conservative Republicans who took the pledge to rid the nation of you, Mr. President?

And oh, wasn't there once a black Congressman from Oklahoma by the name of J.C. Watts?

Wasn't he once supposed to be next in line for a committee chairmanship or

some major role in the Republican
hierarchy?

I guess he was so beloved by his fellow
Republicans that they not only did not
consider him to become one of their
leaders, but they didn't want to intrude
on his busy speaking engagements to
ask him to show up on TV as one of
their chief spokespersons in their
attempts to evict you from the White
House.

And the gay community…do you think
they're going to be with you now that
that "Don't Ask, Don't Tell' repeal is
done…that you have sort of come out in
favor of same sex
marriage/rights/unions?

You do know they have a contingent of
outspoken gay Log Cabin Republicans
in their midst.

I hope they won't be too angry with you
for waiting so long…that too many of
them have not gone over to that group of
gay Republicans…shading their eyes as
they stare off into the sunrise where
John Boehner is astride his white horse?

I was confident that you did feel a little guilty when all these openly gays and advocates for equal rights appeared on TV and said they were disappointed in you.

And didn't you squirm a bit when that West Point officer who happens to speak a much needed Arabic tongue was drummed out of the Army because he dared to stand up for his principles and declared he's gay?

Yeah I get it that you have 'evolved,' that you were once against gay marriages because you bought into the logic that marriage should only be between a man and a woman, but I'm glad you thumbed your nose at McCain and those right wingers and did the right thing.

For a while there Mr. President, I was asking myself what happened to that pen of yours that you can legally use to enact an Executive Order?

But you got it done anyway. Now let's hope those in the media who were so critical of you for not having kept your

promise, will now give you your
'props.'

Just be careful Mr. President. Don't
bank on all those old generals who
normally 'come out' as Republicans
once their days on the battle field end, to
cooperate.

When I listened to those Republicans
say you were weak, hinting that you
would not defend our country, I didn't
lose any sleep wondering if there was a
shred of truth in what they were
packaging for their followers.

Then when you had your special ops
forces send Bin Laden that 'policy
statement' and sent Al-Awalaki a wake
up call with that drone,' and I watched
how your critics half-heartedly gave you
'props,' I knew that they would have to
come up with another angle rather than
simply suggesting you were weak on
defense.

And as sure as I'm the retired, black guy
writing you this letter, they came up
with something to put in those
'medicine bottles' that they're always
selling at those Republican gatherings.

Sure you gave the okay, they were
forced to admit on those TV interviews,
but they reminded all their conservative
diehards that the real credit should go to
the military, not you…that you were
still no Ronald Reagan…that no matter
what decisions you should make
regarding troop withdrawals or
deployment…regardless of any foreign
policy you and your advisors might have
in mind "we should listen to the
generals, not you."

Didn't you already make it clear to one
of your generals that you were the
president; that generals didn't make
foreign polity or go public with their
personal assessments of you and your
brain thrusts?

If I were you I'd be keeping my eyes on
some of these generals; make sure
they're not going to try to sabotage this
repeal .

After all, Mr. President, some of these
guys brag about how when they entered
the military they didn't have to worry
about some gay guy in the next bunk
coming over to kiss them good

night…well, at least they won't come clean on such sensitive issues.

They're never going to go public and admit that at some time while they were in Vietnam, a gay guy actually saved their rear end by taking out some of those Vietcong.

I'm just saying Mr. President, when Senator McCain starts naming those generals who think gays serving and dying for their country defies something their ministers told them was in the Bible, I'd be wary.

This is the same McCain who keeps insisting that you don't get it when it comes to foreign affairs.

Every time there's some atrocity in Syria, Iraq, Pakistan or anti-American sentiment anywhere in the world, McCain wants all Americans to believe that it's because of your failed leadership. He wants them to know that you're being viewed as 'weak,' 'indecisive.'

You see, Mr. President, Senator McCain knows a thing or two about using U.S.

firepower to solve all issues. And he crashed enough fighter aircraft trying to land on an aircraft carrier to know what it's like to face adversity head on.

So when he gets on those news programs and hints that you need to flex America's military might to show those Iranians and Syrians that you mean business, I'm glad you continue to leer at him the way you did during the debates when he tried to convince you that overstaying his welcome at the Hanoi Hilton qualified him as a foreign policy expert.

And just a thought, Mr. President, do you think some of these guys who opposed you on your open policy for gays in the military would have made generals if they had served under that Alexander guy from Macedonia who enjoyed slaughtering his opponents during the day, then snuggling up with his soldiers at night?

Anyway, I hope you're up to the task Mr. President; that you'll be willing to show some of them to the door when they go public and defy you.

How is it anyway, Mr. President, that
these generals don't mind your allies
sending a few thousand troops
(including gays) to help you battle Al-
Qaeda and the Taliban, while asking
their young men and women to subject
themselves to some ridiculous
interrogation of their sexual preferences,
and they want to continue doing so with
U.S. military?

What's bothering a lot of us Mr.
President is that we know you're smart
and that you are capable of reading the
tea leaves.

And don't worry, we're still standing by
you even if others appear to be jumping
ship.

Just a bit of advice, Mr. President. If I
were you…and I realize I can't be…I
would refrain from sending the First
Lady into hostile environments like
NASCAR events.

You see, the people who mainly attend
these races are mostly descendents of
those overall-wearing, tobacco chewing,
'Bubbas' who still recall how the likes

of you forced integration and affirmative action on them.

These are people who can't wait to get to the ballot box to attach their names to any Right Wing Republican who vows to kick you out of the White House.

So if I were advising you, I would remind you that none of those prior Republican presidents who preceded you would not have dared send their wives into 'hostile liberal' territory to convince Democrats that they have something to sell.

Maybe it would be better if you sent the First Lady to the Soul Train Music Awards. That way you would ensure that she would receive a warm reception rather than boos from those NASCAR fanatics.

I know you want to convince those right wingers that you are a 'president of all the people,' but Mr. President, these folks are not going to buy your messages. They want you to know that no matter how much you try to reach across the table to compromise, they're going to stand firm…reject anything that might help you gain a second term.

You can bet on it Mr. President, if Michelle shows up at any event like the Soul Train Music Awards, she's not going to run into any of Reagan or Bush kids. And certainly she's not going to see any of 'Bubba's' off-springs snapping their fingers to Bootsy Collins.

And while I'm on the subject of warning you, you need to make sure that during your campaign the world recognizes that it was this pledge to not raise taxes on the wealthiest 1% that your Republican friends clung to in order to avoid your getting that debt reduction agreement passed by the Super Committee.

Let all America know that while your opponents swear that they are 'listening' to the public when they advocate 'no tax increases on the wealthy,' they fail to mention that polls reflect that the voters aren't in sync with them; that they do want the richest of the rich to pay more taxes.

Make sure you remind them that while your buddy Clinton was president, the rich paid more taxes and the economy did just fine…that it was the Bush tax cuts to the rich that had a negative effect on the economy…that instead of those tax cuts creating jobs, they only resulted in the 'fat cats' lining their pockets and increasing their bottom line…that over the last 30 years, the income growth of the rich has increased some 275% while the rest of America has bumped along with minimum or no increase…that while you continue to target the millionaires and billionaires for those tax increases, the Republicans keep trying to convince the public that you want to raise taxes on EVERYONE!...that the Republicans on the Super Committee admitted that it was the Democrats who refused to 'budge' during the Super Committee debt reduction deliberations; charging that the Democrats refused to concede MORE on domestic spending… simultaneously they admit that they refused to budge one iota on their insistence that there be NO tax hikes on the rich.

And if you're waiting on the media to explain these facts to their audiences, don't hold your breath.

What they want is to adhere to their policy of 'balanced' news…i.e. ensure that none of those Tea Party/Right Wing attacks are hurled in their directions; accusing them of 'biased' reporting by identifying the real culprits whose main political agenda it is to 'defeat Obama.'

But what we hope you won't do is swallow your principles just to appease these Republicans who have illustrated that they are going to cling to their values and not compromise regardless of how much you extend the olive branch.

We listen to the media pundits saying it's now time for you to do more compromising. But when they timidly ask the Republicans what they are willing to compromise on, the Republicans remain rigid, smirk and remind the interviewer that they speak for the 'American people,' and they agree with Boehner and his gang that compromise is a sign of weakness.

Doesn't that kind of suggest to you Mr. President that maybe your opposition has no interest in swallowing their principles; that the only swallowing

they're interested in is watching when
you cave in on your principles?

And I'm sure your media watchers took
note of Congresswoman Maxine
Waters' words of caution uttered at that
August, 2011 Congressional Black
Caucus job fair…when she reminded
you that while she is in agreement with
your coming out with a rural community
job program…all your plans for job
creation…your support for Latinos and
gays…she doesn't understand why you
haven't announced something that will
address the plight of those 16%
unemployed blacks who reside mostly
in urban communities.

And if you know Congresswoman
Waters as some of us who have lived
and worked in Los Angeles do, you
know that she is not going to zip it up
just to avoid aggravating you…that if I
were sitting with you in your Oval
Office I would remind you not to
alienate those blacks who have stood by
you while others were throwing gasoline
on the Tea Party's funeral pyre they're
constructing for your anticipated
departure from the White House.

What the Congresswoman and many of us hope you'll do is go on the offense and start kicking some Tea Party rear ends.

We knew when we voted for you that you were a conciliator who believed there was only one America, but we're hoping you'll understand that to recognize that America is and always has been a diverse community that survives despite its racial and cultural rainbows…that it's okay to accept the reality that there will always be a strain of the population that will never consider you a 'genuine American' simply because you are not white and conservative.

What many of us hope you'll do is resort to realpolitik and stand tall.

We would like to see you be a President whose values and priorities do not waiver in the face of an implacable opposition simply to maintain your image as a conciliator.

The entire world is watching Mr. President to see if you are the strong leader needed to guide America out of its malaise and bring the nation back to global respectability.

People in Europe, Asia, Africa, and Latin America are undecided. They listen to your speeches and they are impressed, but as they watch the Republicans chisel away at your popularity at home, they wonder how long they can continue offering up their resources and young men and women to aid America in its international efforts if America's President seems unwilling to do battle with his foes at home.

The world needs another Roosevelt, Truman, Kennedy, Johnson, or Clinton, and they're waiting for you to show them that you're the man…presidents who saved the world from the Axis…defied the Berlin Blockade and let the world know "The Buck Stops Here"…turned back Soviet missiles…bucked impeachment and fattened American pockets…signed Civil Rights' legislation in face of severe political consequences.

And while some world leaders may be licking their chops, thinking that perhaps the U.S. is on the brink of its demise as the world's super power, they know that it's more wishful thinking than reality.

They have their eyes on your relationship with Israel, not quite sure how far you'll go to broker a peace deal that has eluded your predecessors.

They hear the applause you received in Egypt but they wonder, if we consider realpolitik, whether Al-Qaeda's bomb makers will be deterred simply because you recognize the legitimacy of Islam, or if Palestinian and Iranian map makers suddenly admit that Israel actually exists

They suspect that these Islamic extremists would prefer to see business as usual along the West Bank; a divided Israel, Palestine that aids Al-Qaeda and others in their recruitment of followers willing to strap on bomb belts and take off to meet Allah.

They hear you speak of bringing some of the troops home from Iraq and Afghanistan and they know that the reality is that just like Germany, Japan, and South Korea, America's military will stay the course for many years…realpolitik that too many American's are unwilling to accept.

Now that you have assured all of us that we won't have to listen to any more Bin Laden tapes, and that his top aides are cupping their ears trying to determine if a drone missile is dialing up their name and location…if some special ops guys or CIA operatives are outside their door…and those right wing critics of yours formerly claiming that you didn't have the grit that John Wayne exhibited when he was playing make-believe in all those tough guy Hollywood movies, have been silenced…I think they all know now that while you may smile and give the impression that you're just a stoic intellectual, you don't have a problem unleashing the U.S.'s military might to take out someone on your 'kill list.'

And maybe if, like some of us, these skeptics had watched you sharpening your elbows on the basketball court, they would have realized that you're no cream puff.

IX

So now Mr. President that the American
voters have spoken and returned
Republicans to control of Congress, and
John Boehner, the new Republican
leader in Congress who reminded you
regarding your health care plan…
"We're going to do everything-and I
mean everything-we can do, to kill it,
stop it, slow it down"…is wielding the
gavel that his voters ripped from Nancy
Pelosi's hands…what conciliatory skills
are you going to utilize to coerce him to
water down his vow?

And since it appears that you'll be
facing Governor/Bain Capital profiteer
Mitt Romney come November, I suggest
it's time for you to come out 'smokin'
like old Joe Frazier.

Yes, I did watch the CNN 'impartial'
hosts seeming to rejoice over the voters

sending you a message; reminding you that 'you're out of touch.'

For the better part of two months I listened to the predictions how the Republicans were going to sweep Nancy and her 'liberal' mob out of Congress, and it was all about the President being out of touch; not able to provide jobs, spending too much, too much big government interference, but I didn't get what I thought the media should have done a better job on.

I didn't hear anyone at CNN dig into what was really on the minds of so many Republicans, Independents, and Tea Party supporters who couldn't wait to get to the polls and vote Republican.

I didn't hear enough pundits ask the question… "how much does race play a factor in the strong opposition to President Obama?"

Not that I or anyone would accuse that all those who oppose you do so simply because they are racist or because they can't tolerate seeing a black face emerge when they hear 'Hail To The Chief.' But to imply that none of those folks are uncomfortable with having a black president is ludicrous.

Your friend Wanda Sikes understands it, but then maybe her blasts from reality are a bit too discomforting.

Well then, maybe if you're still not sure, tune in sometime to that comedian/TV host Bill Maher who wrote you that $1 million check.

He just cuts right to the chase and calls a white sheet like he sees it, and he's not afraid to state publicly that much of this 'hatred' of you is based on one prime factor…RACE!

And oh, Mr. President, wasn't it the scholarly Sarah Palin who told you that the American voters were going to say "You blew it…we gave you two years to fulfill your promise of making sure that our economy starts roaring back to life again?"

Then there was the other 'great communicator,' one Patrick Buchanan who declared there is… "a growing perception that Obama is biased."

Or better yet, Mr. Glen Beck who agreed but went even further, charging you have… "a deep-seated hatred for white people or the white culture."

So, President Obama, tell me, does this mean that all those years while growing up you had a 'deep-seated' hatred for your mother…your grandparents?

Yes Mr. President, they're rejoicing.

And after you had your press conference the day following the 2010 congressional elections, the Republican CNN contributor, Alex Castellanos, was quick to point out that the American public and his Republican /Tea Party/Independents get it and you don't…that you need to admit that your policies have failed..

The other Republicans chimed in, boasting that this was proof that you still didn't get it; that you were still unwilling to admit that everything that plagued America over the last 20 or so years was all your fault.

One David Gergen, who always boasts that he served not only during

Republican administrations but the
Clinton White House as well, had to be
interrupted when he began a tirade on
how it was a bad time for you to be
running off to Asia.

This, by the way, Mr. President, is the
same Mr. Gergen who would rather
spend most of his time reminiscing (like
other Republicans) on the 'good old
Reagan years'…the one who never
explains exactly what condition the U.S.
economy was in during and after
Reagan rode off into the sunset…rather
than explaining the Clinton magic that
his friend George W. rejected.

It might have slipped his mind that this
Asian trip of yours and your attending
the G-20 summit was a trip once before
postponed, or that it was on your
schedule before the mid-term elections.

What Mr. Gergen, this popular CNN
guest known for his 'even handed'
analysis and supposed 'independence,'
needed the viewers to sense, was that
once again you were out of touch with
'real' America…that instead of
attending to foreign affairs and flying
off with a group of U.S. business

executives to try to encourage Asians to
be a bit more receptive to buying
American, you should have been
knocking on Mr. Boehner's office door
and begging for an opportunity to speak
with him...to show the American people
that you had gotten the message and was
willing and ready to compromise/kiss
a...

You see Mr. President, you're not
supposed to know what's good for the
country, and you're supposed to admit
that every program you enacted was
detrimental to the nation.

What right have you to suggest that
without your bailing out industries the
economy would have spiraled even
further down...by providing health care
for previous denied persons, and
extending access...by getting 'Don't
Ask, Don't Tell' repealed...getting your
arms treaty passed despite McCain and
his buddies accusing you of 'caving' in
to the communists...was something
positive for Americans...that no one
needs to wonder anymore whether Bin
Laden is in a cave or on a yacht in the
Mediterranean...whether Al-Alawaki's
hate America/kill Americans e-mails

will again motivate Americans to become traitors?

And would you please refrain from reminding 'real' Americans that it was that Bush guy who was responsible for getting the U.S. into this economic quagmire in the first place.

Haven't you been listening to CNN advocating that it's time to move on, for you to take full blame for the nation's economic woes and unemployment …that Americans don't what to hear about the past, only what you're going to do to make their lives better?

Oh yes, Mr. President, these are the same 'impartial' journalist who studied history in school so they could understand that in order to move forward we needed to know where we've been.

Except that axiom doesn't apply to you Mr. President.

Remember, you were elected to perform astonishing feats, not give us lessons.

It was the likes of John Kennedy who could remind us to not ask what our country can do for us, but what we could do for our country.

But your name's Obama. Half of your ancestors come from some bush country in Africa, not Camelot.

X

But trust me Mr. President, your true
base is still behind you.

Just because a large segment of voters
are on the attack or have bailed water
out of their 'Independent' canoes and
raised their flags of surrender in face of
the Republican/Tea Party/Romney
periscope they see beneath the water,
some of us still are on course with you.

We know the battle you're waging and
we know it is difficult.

We notice how your hair has taken on a
tint of gray and we realize that also
comes with the job of being the leader
of the world's superpower.

The problem is Mr. President, some of
those less political, kind of figured that
when they watched you take the oath of

office that somehow you could wave some kind of magic wand and bring sudden prosperity to their lives.

How many discussions, even arguments did I continue to have with friends as I tried to define realpolitik and differentiate between what we wish and what we're likely to get.

You see Mr. President, all those years of feeling disenfranchised; not sensing that our votes could make a difference…that we were being taken for granted…that no one really cared…had left too many black folk sitting on the curb wondering if life in an emerging new African nation might not be the answer.

Remember, lots of black folk had gone through the 60s and 70s trying on their dashikis and letting their Afros blossom; imagining going 'home' and being received with open arms by their African brothers.

But while it may have worked for a few black notables, most returned to the States aware that despite all the revolutions and African state independences, we were still just plain old Americans; that a black born in Ghana is not the same as a black born in Los Angeles' Watts.

It dawned on many that our forefathers had sacrificed too much for us to pull up stakes, leave and abandon the fight.

And now that we see you in the White House and a few black multi-millionaires being highlighted from time to time, we've imagined that maybe white America senses a bit of pride in having lowered its racial barriers and accept Black America as a vital partner.

But then when we watched them show their disrespect and that South Carolina Congressman call you a 'liar' during your State of the Union address before the joint bodies of the Senate and Congress, we realized that it wasn't that we had achieved so much, but rather that it was mostly US who were glad that times had indeed changed for the good.

Then we were jolted back into reality as we watched the emergence of the Tea Party with their hate-filled signs and

innuendoes, and the shifting of love for
you from the media.

We frowned as we listened to CNN
announce polls revealing that some
whites insisted you were a Muslim…
that despite your birth certificate to the
contrary, you were not an American…
that maybe you had attended schools in
Indonesia taught my Islamic radicals
bent on destroying America…that you
couldn't be a Christian if your father
was a Muslim, since a child born to a
Muslim father MUST adopt his father's
religion.

That's when we began to take notice of
the real changing America

Many of us born to the generation
before you that had witnessed the
assassinations of the two Kennedys and
Dr. Martin Luther King and all those
civil rights fighters, began to worry
about your safety when we learned that
there was chatter on the internet hinting
that maybe it was time for you to meet
your death in like fashion.

I, I'm sure like many of my black peers
who had spent time in newsrooms and

TV studios, worried as we watched the shifting sands of the network and cable news programming.

Where had gone the accolades, the kind words regarding the welcome change in America's political and social arena?

Suddenly it appeared that editors and news/program directors were running for cover; under attack from the irate Republicans suddenly out of the White House.

The campaign had begun. Rush Limbaugh was on the attack.

Everything that you preached…that there was only one America…that the country had achieved something historic…that the world was clapping in approval on seeing America emerge from a nation of historical exclusion, electing a black president…was there for the world to hear and see..

Oh, but the Republicans would have none of it.

Since George Washington, white America had simply assumed that no

matter how many blacks they saw now
dominating their collegiate and
professional sports, music…no matter
Oprah Winfrey, Denzel Washington,
General Adam Clayton Powell, the
country had now gone too far.

With Mexicans and other foreigners
'invading' here-to-fore mostly white
towns…Asians topping the list of
university scholars as they gained a
disproportionate number of
admissions…blacks climbing ladders
and becoming more visible in leadership
roles…predictions that with increasing
child births among mostly recent
Mexican immigrants, America would
soon see current minorities as the
majority population…and now a black
president!

It was time for action!

White America needed to 'take back'
the country that they had always been
led to believe was rightfully theirs.

Wasn't it their forefathers who had
braved the Atlantic crossing, landed on
Plymouth Rock and killed off the
Indians?

Didn't they enact the Monroe Doctrine
that made the Western Hemisphere
America's sphere of influence?

Hadn't some of their forefathers once
enslaved ancestors of many of the same
blacks now competing for a slice of the
American dream?

Wasn't it their grandparents and parents
who had fought the two great wars that
saved Europe and Asia from evil men
like the Kaiser, Hitler, and Tojo?

Didn't they put a man on the moon?

So what right did these upstart
minorities have usurping white power?

Hell, whites say, they're tired of being
reminded about the many contributions
blacks have made to enhance America.

No matter that black slaves, with their
'free' labor had aided in boosting
America's economic growth…that they
had been doing so long before the great
majority of whites stepped off the wharf
at Ellis Island.

They, blacks, may have been fighting
and dying to protect America's freedom
and maintain its unity since the
British/American War…they may have
been responsible for major inventions
that aided in America's development as
an industrialized world power…many
may have survived the overt
discrimination and Jim Crow laws
designed to keep them as second-
class…they may now dominate many
sectors of America and are visible in
virtually every nook and cranny of
American life and success, but no
matter, they are still not white!...say
some now feeling threatened by the
growing tide of non-whites.

So, you see Mr. President, for many of
those who now so strongly oppose you
and hope to paint you with the dark
brush of doom, you have become the
symbol of what they feel has gone
wrong with America.

They cringe when they see you skipping
up the stairs to board Air Force One
…they curse when they see foreign
heads of state honor and acknowledge
you as leader of the free world…it
bothers them to be reminded of your

achievements at Harvard, especially
given your rather humble beginning.

Their wives don't know what to make of
the first lady and her own achievements,
and her class and beauty, given they
grew up admiring the likes of Mamie
Eisenhower, Pat Nixon, Nancy Reagan,
and Barbara and Laura

And they still can't figure out exactly
what kind of black you really are.

You see, while they did open their
hearts, many white Americans realize
that since their slave master forefathers
took a liking to their dark-hued female
slaves, 'coloreds' and 'negroes' with
featured like yours have long dawned
America's landscape.

Fact was that while these 'creole' and
'mulatto' types existed, most whites
paid little heed to their racial status;
only that if they had an inkling of
'negro' blood, then they were 'negroes,'
nothing more.

Now you appear on every magazine
cover, TV network, newspaper front
page with your mixed-race features.

And while you do occasionally bring up
issues of race, you don't appear to be
threatening.

Unlike Jesse Jackson and the Reverend
Al Sharpton, you don't appear on TV
reminding them that racism still exists in
America...about how they marched with
Dr. King and ducked Bull Conner's
dogs and nightsticks.

No, Mr. President you talked about
moving on to another chapter of
American history; reminding everyone
that we were all Americans.

Sure, that worked for a while, that is
until those 'Independents' started having
to explain to their right wing Republican
friends and business and NRA card
carrying associates why they had opted
to vote for you instead of Senator
McCain.

You see Mr. President you
accomplished something that I'm sure
you had no intention of doing.

You provided impetus for those closet
doors to swing open once again.

Suddenly those irate Republicans and
those 'used to be' Republicans turned
'Independents' reverted back to
sentiments stored away since Kennedy
reminded them that it was morally
wrong to discriminate, and Johnson
signed that 'misguided' civil rights
legislation making it costly to openly
discriminate…since that 'Slick Willie'
Clinton entered the White House talking
'black' and seemingly comfortable with
a black hand draped over his shoulder or
his over a black woman's.

Now there was no holding them back.

You, Mr. President are the reason they
decided it was time to have a Tea Party,
and it had nothing to do with the taxes
without representation that drove the
folks in Boston to throw their party.

And while they saw no need to circle the
Bush wagon with their rallies when he
blew the Clinton surplus and sent the
U.S. economy into a nose dive, now it
was time to round up the troops.

CNN and other media experts shrugged
them off at first, but when the attacks
came, charging the media with being

'liberal college educated know it alls'
swooning over this President Obama,
they quickly got the message..

So instead of sending their reporters out
to expand on the Obama mystique, now
news directors and editors wanted their
reporters to see if there was another side
to Obama that perhaps they had
overlooked…anything that would allow
them to elude the right wing arrows
being fired at them.

Was he smoking something other than a
Winston when he sneaked off with Bo,
claiming that he was taking the dog for a
walk?

Where was this school in Indonesia?

And what about his father…did the
African father have a history of anti-
Americanism that might have rubbed off
on his son?

Keep digging on that minister in
Chicago who must have had some
influence on the President's mind set.

Maybe he is an 'elitist.' After all, he did

go to Harvard and doesn't speak like he
spent much time in the ghetto.

And what about his wife? Are we sure
she made her way through college and
into a major law firm without some
illegal affirmative action benefits
…something that might qualify as
reverse discrimination?

And what about his days in the Illinois
state senate? There must be something
questionable there that allowed him to
move up to the U.S. Senate so rapidly.

Now instead of looking for balance
reporting regarding the President, the
media needed to revert to a series of
tidbits they could throw out to appease
the Tea Party and Republicans and
deflect the accusations.

Was it wise for the President to go out
on a night on the town in New York
with his wife? Did he use public funds?

What kind of deals did the White House
make with British Petroleum? Was
Obama doing all he could to stop the oil
spill? Why wasn't he using the
expertise of NASA? After all if we

could land a craft on Mars why couldn't
we stop an oil spill?

Why was the President and his family
vacationing in Massachusetts instead of
in the Gulf, assuring American's that the
beaches were safe? Why wasn't the
President spending more time in the
region pressing BP to speed up its clean
up efforts and get those checks out
quicker?

Just this past August, the Republicans
explained that while Bush and Reagan
did take many vacations at their places
in Crawford, Texas and Santa Barbara,
California, clearing brush and riding
horses, unlike you, they were still
attending to the nation's business, not
living the 'life of the rich and famous'
up in some snobbish Massachusetts
town while the U.S. economy was
tanking and people were in desperate
need of employment.

American needed to stretch its
imagination and believe that Bush and
Reagan were whacking weeds and
sitting in the saddle at the same time
they were busy on their lap tops

directing soldiers in Iraq and CIA
operatives in Nicaragua.

But then I was having a bit of difficulty
trying to recall some legislation or
Presidential Orders emanating from
Crawford or Santa Barbara that ended
up on the dockets of the Senate or
Congress; proof that Bush and Reagan
were actually working in their vacation
site offices rather than relaxing and
enjoying their favorite pastimes.

Sometimes I forget that as far as these
Republican 'friends' of yours are
concerned, you don't deserve to
vacation with your family since you
didn't have friends/wealthy family to
bequeath you with a ranch where you
could whisk away in Air Force One and
have the media camped out across the
road hoping to capture you in those
photo-ops chopping wood or pretending
you were John Wayne, while Wayne
was all the time pretending he was
someone else..

They wanted to paint you as some social
snob who preferred dining out with your
family at a restaurant where a maitre-de
welcomed guests with reservations,

rather than riding around in a pickup or galloping on a horse.

Now I guess what we are supposed to surmise from this comparison is that you're simply 'out of touch' with the American public; that Reagan and Bush knew exactly what we all wanted…that the great majority of us preferred ending up with more debt and little improvement in our per capita income, while the rich got fatter.

And of course your opponents decided it was time to give your wife her comeuppance as well.

Instead of worrying about fat teenagers, maybe the First Lady should have her own kids down on the Gulf with pails and rakes.

And the media news director wanted their reporters to check on this Chicago minister again. Surely there must be some evidence showing Obama sitting in front of his 'guru' Reverend Jeremiah while the minister was spouting those nasty things about America.

And what's the President doing expressing his personal views about some black Cambridge professor being arrested for entering his own house?

Was he playing the race card when he said the white cop was wrong?

Check to see if maybe this professor guy has some Muslim connection…maybe the FBI has something on him in Hoover's old files.

Wasn't that some kind of 'black' thing, that handshake Obama and Chavez exchanged that time at the U.N.?

See if there's something in Obama's past writings indicating he admires this anti-American Venezuelan 'communist.'

Make sure you listen carefully when he attends those NAACP and Urban League conventions…look for some anti-white statements.

What ties does the President have to the 'radical left wing' Acorn group? See if there's a money trail from Obama and the Democrats to Acorn.

And this firing of this black woman that
the Department of Agriculture Secretary
says he was solely responsible for…did
Obama order it?

Yes Mr. President, you not only brought
them out of the closet where they kept
their white robes and hoods, but you got
the white media thinking also.
Did they want to have to do something
they felt uncomfortable doing…going to
bat for a black president and face the
wrath of Sarah Palin and Rush
Limbaugh?

So Mr. President, because you had
changed the flavor of the White House,
the media needed to reconsider.

After all, weren't they white also?

Deep down didn't they understand how
the Republicans, Tea Party, and
'Independents' might be feeling?

You see, they too felt a little uneasy
staring up at this new president during
White House news conferences.

Oh sure, they might have attended an
occasional social event where they

shook hands with some black
personality.

And they may have rooted for some
blacks during college sporting events,
but they never had to address them as
'Mr. President,' or explain to their
conservative brother-in-law why they
raised their clenched fist when Jeter
drove in the winning run to beat the
hated Red Sox.

And as I watched this media charade of
'impartial' reporting, it reminded me of
my old, but brief career in journalism.

I reflected on how so many of my white
peers in the newsroom had themselves
looked in that mirror…how most had
signed that petition to prevent more
minorities coming to the daily.

It reminded me that while there may be
'liberals' on TV and in newsrooms,
when they have to make a tough choice
of displaying support for things black in
face of their white peers' opposition,
most will do what comes naturally.

They take a swallow of bourbon and
resign themselves to the fact that while

they might not agree with everything the right wing and Tea Party personalities expound, they do have one historical commonality…they're white.

And what they conclude, Mr. President, is that if getting along within their social circles requires avoiding any accusation that they are 'liberal' supporters of a black president, then it's best to stick with their cultural roots.

It's not that these 'liberal/impartial' media personalities have become racists Mr. President, it's simply that it's becoming burdensome to wear the 'left' label anymore.

They see the train light in the tunnel and they sense that John Boehner's gavel looks more like a hatchet, and that your arch rival in the Senate, Mitch McConnell has his foot out, waiting for Harry Reid to pass by.

These media personalities are slick Mr. President. They won't openly admit it but I think they are preparing for your downfall.

No matter that giving the rich tax breaks

under Bush did little more than add to
their (the richest of the rich) investments
and bank accounts…not adding jobs in
the U.S. but maybe a few in Asia and
Mexico…the media folks are not going
to spend much time letting their viewers
and listeners know that those tax cuts to
fat cats actually cost the U.S. billions in
tax dollars that could have reduced the
Bush deficit.

And they're certainly not going to take
one on the chin for you by explaining
that if these tax cuts only added to the
nation's financial woes under Bush; just
how is it possible they can benefit the
nation now?

No Mr. President, this has nothing to do
with making life better for those 95% of
Americans who can't afford their kids'
college tuitions.

This is all about those
Republican/Independents/Tea Party
folks openly challenging your power.

They want to show their supporters that
they can stop you from doing anything
that might ensure your sitting behind
that Oval Office desk for another four

years.

They want their county back Mr.
President and you're an obstacle!

That's why those Republican mouth
pieces Mitch McConnell, John Boehner,
and Eric Cantor let you know that
they're going to 'block virtually all
legislation' until you agree to extend
those Bush tax cuts.

And that's exactly why Cantor went on
CNN and proudly announced that
during their little sit down meal with
you, you admitted that you had not
previously 'reached out enough' to his
party.

But maybe I missed something being
down here in Mexico with limited media
access, but since I didn't see a response
from your team, explaining that it has
been the Republicans who are the ones
not extending a hand...that it was been
the Republicans that thought it best if
their leader Mr. McConnell opt to speak
to a group of right wing zealots rather
than RSVP for that first invite you
tendered.

You see Mr. President, these guys feel
that the voters 'repudiated' your agenda
and now you're ignoring that 'fact.'

Even when the Supreme Court upheld
what the Republicans like to demean as
'Obama Care,' they still accuse you of
'ramming through' health care
legislation that 'nobody wants.

They are going to fight you all the way
Mr. President, as they attempt to paint
your health care plan as a 'tax,' not a
penalty for those some 1% of Americans
who can afford to but prefer not to buy
health insurance.

What does it matter that more than 30
million Americans will be able to have
health coverage? Heck, most of your
opponents have their health insurance,
and as far as they are concerned, those
30 millions who will benefit from your
'socialism' are probably non-
Republican whites/poor/minorities who
are most likely going to vote for you.

And no matter how many times they are
reminded that most of the world's
developed nations have some type of
universal health care that provides, in

many cases better service, at a cheaper cost, the Republicans are going to insist that your 'Obama Care' is going to bankrupt the country…that it is already driving up the cost of health insurance.

And if you're waiting for the media to explain that you are not the CEO of any health provider; that it is the insurance industry that continues to expand the cost of health care, not you, then I suggest you get one of those 'mojo' sticks to help you understand your dilemma.

What you're going to have to do Mr. President is spend more of your ad dollars outlining the facts. Every time the Republicans send someone on TV to attack 'Obama Care,' don't be like your buddy Senator Kerry and let them get away with tainting you with that liar's brush.

You need to be on the attack, not worry that the media will surely brand you as the bad guy for accusing Romney and his gang of distorting your message…for getting into Romney's bag of tricks and tossing out some 'smelly' laundry for the voters to see.

It's all about who has the 'cajones' Mr.
President.

You can let the Republicans stay on the
offense with their rebuffing tactics that
make it appear you're on the defensive,
or you can come out with your own 'two
minute, no huddle drill' offense that
prevents them from running out the
clock…that can get you in position for a
field goal…a touchdown…maybe a k.o.

What you need to do Mr. President is
assure even your doubters that you're no
push over conciliator…that you're not
afraid to take McConnell and Boehner
one on one…that Romney better be
ready for a frontal attack.

Just like you don't seem to back down
when you're going five on five with
your hoop friends, most folks want to
see you hit some three pointers on those
right wing loud mouths.

Isn't that what Jordan used to do to quiet
the hostile crowds Mr. President?
Now remember Mr. President, those
media guys and gals watch their polls
and they figure since the majority

of white voters have jumped ship and
are swimming in the direction of the Tea
Party/Romney attack submarine, that
perhaps they too need to change course.

So now that even the media has decided
that sipping a spot of tea seems more
American than slurping Starbucks latte,
then who's left in your corner?

Like Old Faithful, black Americans,
who voted 95 % for you, some young
whites, and the majority of other
minorities are with you.

All they're asking is that you take a little
time and look in their direction once in a
while and raise your fist to let them
know that you also feel their pain.

While I have spent a great deal of my
life among other members of America's
melting pot, I don't profess to be able to
tell you exactly what messages you can
send their way to keep them faithful.

Maybe you'll be getting a letter in
Spanish or Mandarin soon.
What I think I can say though is that
most Black Americans look for certain

indicators to know that you know they're out there…maybe seeing you on CNN talking 'smack' with some of the old hands at the neighborhood black barber shop…sending a shout out to that old friend of mine, Willie Brown, then talking politics while you two ride around in his Porsche…strolling down Crenshaw Boulevard in Los Angeles with Magic Johnson while he gives you a tour of his business empire…seeing maybe another black face sitting around your kitchen cabinet…celebrating Black History Month with gusto…shooting a few hoops and talking 'smack' with Charles Barkley (now that ought to convince both whites and blacks you're on to something risqúe).

And Mr. President I know you saw that actor Wesley Snipes being shuttled off to jail for not paying all his taxes, but what about those other guys who tried to get away with not paying billions, but ended up getting a slap on the wrist and an ankle bracelet?

You think maybe Mr. Eric Holder can have some of his people look into it…maybe pass a note to you to add Wesley to your pardon list?

Hey, Mr. President, the brother has paid enough taxes over the years to keep even Congress in perks.

Can't he get a little love?

We're not asking a lot Mr. President. Just that we feel with you in the White House we can be assured that we're not being taken for granted once again after we cast deciding votes to get folks elected.

Sure, we understand that issues like immigration are important, but we kind of figure that urban problems are more pressing since they've been kicking black folk in the butt from the time they began migrating from those Southern plantations.

We stood with you when you went to bat for illegal immigrants and said they needed a path to citizenship, and we didn't raise our voices in protest while others demonstrated in the streets, waved foreign flags, and demanded 'rights' that maybe we thought they were being a bit hasty in asking for.

Even when you sent your lawyers from
the Attorney General's office down to
Arizona to remind Governor Brewer
that racial profiling was un-American;
that issues of immigration should be
handled by the Federal Government, we
could see what you were trying to do.

But a few of us took note that when a
number of major cities decided to enact
laws to make their cites 'sanctuaries' for
illegal immigrants, we wondered why
you didn't insist that such local actions
infringed on the Federal Government's
role regarding issues of immigration just
as in Arizona.

Then in mid-August, 2011, following
planned demonstrations by Latinos and
their supporters, protesting your
Administration's deportation of illegal
immigrants (most convicted or charged
with criminal activities), you decided to
delay some deportation and review the
deportation actions 'case by case.'

I'm just saying Mr. President, there
seems to be a lot of politicking going on
these days that reeks of placating some
special interests while wanting some of
the rest of us to be patient, 'stop

complaining,' and understand that
we're all Americans, not separate racial
classes; that your efforts to improve the
economy and create jobs will eventually
trickle down to bolster all Americans in
need, regardless of race or locale.

Yet, I'm just saying Mr. President, it
seems that when those special interest
groups who gave you 60 % of their vote
that didn't approach the total black vote
you received, are getting more bang for
their vote than black folks; that when
they complain you seem to be listening.

But like Congresswoman Maxine
Waters reminded, maybe it's time you
put some of those urban dwellers on
your list of things to do; let blacks in
Chicago, New York, New Orleans,
Atlanta, and Dallas know that you feel
their pain and that you're going to send
a little love their way even if those
Republicans/Tea Party folks attack you
for 'playing the race card.'

Sure, I thought taking those big, fancy,
million dollar black busses to those
Midwest towns was smart politics, but I
didn't understand why you couldn't
have taken a detour to the West and

South sides of Chicago and delivered one of your speeches on the state of the nation as well.

So Mr. President, I'm writing this little letter to let you know that while I'm with you through thick and thin and I do feel your pain, I want you to understand that I may not be in the majority on this one.

I want you to be aware that there are still lots of wolves out there in sheep's clothing; people who claim they are ready for you but in fact can't wait until they see someone with different features and skin tone sitting in the Oval Office.

You need to be cautious Mr. President as you embark upon your new strategy of conciliation; as you try to entice those right wing Republicans/Independents/ Tea Party folks to join you in rebuilding America.

And I wouldn't spend to much time worrying about that 'old buddy' of yours, Herman Cain, and his new radio talk show scheduled to kick off in 2013. His cover has already been blown. Even those die-hard Obama haters who

feigned love for him earlier, now realize
that he's hoping to sell a few more
books and get on that 'gravy train'
speakers' list, so that he can travel
around the country and tell people how
'black' you are…remind them that he
'loves' being a black Republican who
can show America that he hasn't been
'brainwashed' like the other 99% Black
Americans who read their history of
'who did what' to defend the cause of
civil rights, and who opposed.

And make sure when you put that car in
drive and try to get it out of the ditch
that Mitt Romney all those white folks
standing there with their hands in their
pockets haven't filled that ditch with
quick sand.
And if I were sitting behind that Oval
Desk, waiting for the new Republican
led Congress to start hacking away at all
my programs , I'd make sure I had
enough veto pens ready.

As a matter of fact, if you'd like I can
bring some with me when I come. But
then of course you'll have to make sure
the 'Made In China' doesn't show when
the TV cameras are on.

Anyway, the best of luck to you Mr. President. I'll be down here in Mexico rooting for you.

And the next time I'm in the area, maybe the two of us can get together over some ribs, potato salad, and baked beans, and a cold beer, while I fill you in on the reality that remains America.

So Mr. President, I can only tell you that I wish you well during the next few years as you decide which course you're going to take.

Maybe while you're busy contemplating, it's possible America is thinking it's not yet ready for a non-white American president to gush about his ethnic roots.

Sure the newly elected Senator Marco Rubio from Florida can go public and tell his supporters how proud he is of his Cuban-American roots; that he will always be the son of immigrants.

But then white voters can sort of relate to him. It's not like he looks like that dark Cuban friend of mine, Tito Fuentes!

Maybe there is a double standard when it comes to being a black president.

Perhaps if some of your relatives in Kenya had showed up and stood beside you as you took the oath of office, there might have been an even more rapid negative reaction to you taking the car over to Pennsylvania Avenue with all those white 'liberal' reporters and their camera crews tripping over each other trying to get a close up for the evening news. .

But hopefully the day will come when the next non-white presidential candidate can talk about the influence of his black, Latino, or Asian ancestry without concern for white backlash.

Hopefully Mr. President the sacrifices you make today will ease the acceptability of others surely to follow.

I can just picture in the future, for example, a young black president who gets elected and takes a trip on Air Force One to visit a southern plantation where his ancestors once toiled in slavery, and having the media there with their camera crews, sobbing as they listen to his stories of historical racial debasement.

No matter what those die hard opponents of yours are trying to do to derail your administration, Mr. President, you have proven that in less than two years you have achieved beyond even your most ardent supporters expectations.

I salute you for a job well done. I'm proud to say I lived to witness this 'miracle' on Pennsylvania Avenue.

Oh well, I'd better check myself before I get carried away with my dreams of a changing America.

Like I said Mr. President, I'll give you a holler the next time I'm in the neighborhood.

Until then, stay cool and watch your back.

Yours truly…..